PAINTER'S QUICK REFERENCE

Cats & Dogs

EDITORS OF NORTH LIGHT BOOKS

NORTH LIGHT BOOKS
CINCINNATI, OHIO
www.artistsnetwork.com

Painter's Quick Reference: Cats & Dogs. Copyright © 2007 by North Light Books. Manufactured in China. All rights reserved. It is permissible for the purchaser to paint the designs contained herein and sell them at fairs, bazaars and craft shows. No other part of this book may be reproduced in any form or by any electronic or mechanical means, including information storage and retrieval systems, without permission in writing from the publisher, except by a reviewer, who may quote brief passages in a review. The content of this book has been thoroughly reviewed for accuracy. However, the contributors and publisher disclaim any liability for any damages, losses or injuries that may result from the use or misuse of any product or information presented herein. It is the purchaser's responsibility to read and follow all instructions and warnings on all product labels. Published by North Light Books, an imprint of F+W Publications, Inc., 4700 East Galbraith Road, Cincinnati, Ohio 45236. (800) 289-0963. First edition.

Distributed in Canada by Fraser Direct
100 Armstrong Avenue
Georgetown, ON, Canada L7G5S4

Distributed in the U.K. and Europe by David & Charles
Brunel House, Newton Abbot, Devon TQ12 4PU, England Tel: (+44) 1626 323200, Fax: (+44) 1626 323319
Email: postmaster@davidandcharles.co.uk

Distributed in Australia by Capricorn Link
P.O. Box 704, Windsor, NSW 2756 Australia

Other fine North Light Books are available from your local bookstore, art supply store or direct from the publisher.

11 10 09 08 07   5 4 3 2 1

Library of Congress Cataloging-in-Publication Data
Painter's quick reference : cats & dogs / editors of North Light Books.
          p. cm.
     Includes index.
     ISBN-13: 978-1-58180-859-9 (hardcover : alk. paper)
     ISBN-10: 1-58180-859-3 (hardcover : alk. paper)
     ISBN-13: 978-1-58180-860-5 (pbk. : alk. paper)
     ISBN-10: 1-58180-860-7 (pbk. : alk. paper)
     1. Cats in art. 2. Dogs in art. 3. Painting-Technique I. North Light Books (Firm) II. Title: Cats & dogs. III. Title: Cats & dogs.

  ND1380.P34 2007
  751.45'43297--dc22

                    2006046725

Editors: Holly Davis and Stefanie Laufersweiler
Designer: Karla Baker
Interior Layout Artist: Anna Lubrecht
Production Coordinator: Greg Nock

Metric Conversion Chart

to convert	to	multiply
Inches	Centimeters	2.54
Centimeters	Inches	0.4
Feet	Centimeters	30.5
Centimeters	Feet	0.03
Yards	Meters	0.9
Meters	Yards	1.1
Sq. Inches	Sq. Centimeters	6.45
Sq. Centimeters	Sq. Inches	0.16
Sq. Feet	Sq. Meters	0.09
Sq. Meters	Sq. Feet	10.8
Sq. Yards	Sq. Meters	0.8
Sq. Meters	Sq. Yards	1.2
Pounds	Kilograms	0.45
Kilograms	Pounds	2.2
Ounces	Grams	28.3
Grams	Ounces	0.035

Introduction

When you're in a hurry for painting help, here's the book to come to for ideas, instructions and inspiration.

Nothing is more satisfying for the animal lover and artist than capturing the unique likeness and charming personality of a beloved pet on paper or canvas. Whether your intended subject is a particularly observant tuxedo cat or a playful bunch of Labrador retriever puppies, this easy-to-use reference will quickly show you how to paint every feature and distinctive characteristic of a variety of popular cats and dogs. In addition to separate sections on these two groups of animals, a special section devoted to details ensures that you will re-create not only the essence of your pet but the characteristics that distinguish it.

Here eighteen different artists share their painting secrets and expertise in over forty clear step-by-step demonstrations and valuable "Artist's Comment" insights that are sure to give you exactly what you need. Refresh your skills by becoming reacquainted with fundamental painting techniques, or indulge in your adventurous side and explore new ones. And with painting instruction for three major mediums—acrylic, watercolor and oil—you not only gain advice and tips for your primary medium, but for other mediums you may want to try.

Do you want to learn how to render the glassy brilliance of a tabby's eyes? The long, wavy, silky ears of a cocker spaniel? The regal pose of a German shorthaired pointer? The colorful coat of a tortoiseshell cat? The steps are easier than you think, and they are all within these pages. Simply turn the page, and start painting!

Table of Contents

Cats

Some cats can be classified by breed or type, but what commonly separates one from the next are the markings on its fur and its personality, which unveils itself through the cat's actions. Here we will look at cats of various coats in different states of activity, from still profile to playful pose.

Black Cat

KAREN HUBBARD

MEDIUM: *Acrylic*

COLORS: **Delta Ceramcoat:** *Autumn Brown • Black • Butter Yellow • Dusty Plum • Old Parchment • Pine Green • Purple Smoke • Storm Grey*

BRUSHES: *Pure red sable round no. 1 • script liner no. 1 • flat nos. 6, 12 & ¾-inch (19mm) (Unless otherwise specified, use large brushes to paint large areas and smaller ones for small areas.)*

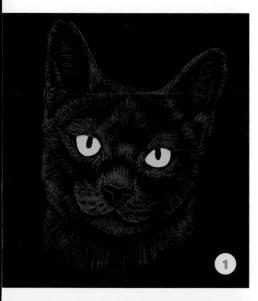

1 Base the Eyes and Begin the Fur

Basecoat the irises with two coats of Butter Yellow. Base the pupils with Black. Paint fur strokes of Autumn Brown inside the ears. Then paint the rest of the fur with Storm Grey fur strokes.

2 Shade the Eyes, Continue the Fur & Begin the Nose

Shade around the pupils and the tops of the irises with a float of Pine Green. Paint a second layer of fur with Purple Smoke fur strokes. Use a flat brush to float the same color around the nostrils and lower edge of the nose.

3 Shade the Eyes, Highlight the Fur and Add Whiskers

Shade again around the pupils and the tops of the irises with a float of Black. Shade the lower edge of the irises with a narrow float of Autumn Brown. Highlight the light (left) side of the cat with Dusty Plum fur strokes. Also highlight a little on the edge of the right ear, on the front corner of the right eye and on the right side of the muzzle, next to the nose. Paint the whiskers on the left with Dusty Plum and on the right with Purple Smoke.

4 Highlight the Eyes and Shade the Entire Cat

(See the completed painting on the opposite page.) Paint a secondary highlight of reflected light in the eyes after predampening the surface. The right eye highlight is Purple Smoke; the left eye is a mix of Purple Smoke + Dusty Plum (1:1). Predampen the left eye between the lower edge and the pupil and add a touch of Old Parchment to brighten. Then add highlight dots of Old Parchment to both eyes. To give the cat a shaded effect, wash over the entire right side with transparent Black, including the eye.

artist's comment

- The fur-stroke technique I refer to in the instructions is done with a flattened round sable brush, slightly thinned paint and very short overlapping brushstrokes.
- The technique of "floating" color is used to create shading or highlights. To sideload your brush for floating color, dip the flattened brush into clean water and blot off the excess. Dip one side of the bristles into the paint, then stroke the brush on the palette until you have a soft blend of color on your bristles that graduates from color on the loaded side to clean water on the other. The color on the loaded side needs to be transparent so that the fur strokes show through. When applied to the painting, the color will be strongest at the edge of the area painted and fade to nothing into the area.

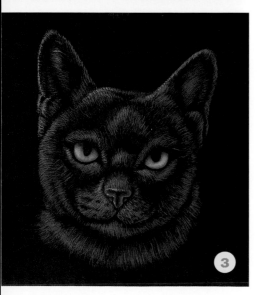

Cat in Window

PAT WEAVER

MEDIUM: *Watercolor*

COLORS: **Da Vinci:** *Aureolin (Mixture)* • *Permanent Rose* • *Ultramarine Blue* • **Holbein:** *Peach Black* • **Shiva Casein:** *Titanium White*

BRUSHES: **Loew-Cornell:** *Series 7020 Golden Taklon Ultra round nos. 10 & 14 (Unless otherwise specified, use large brushes to paint large areas and smaller ones for small areas.)*

artist's comment

I walked into the bedroom, saw Kitty Boy on the window sill and grabbed my camera. Later I made the sketch on the left, choosing the head as the obvious center of interest and placing it accordingly. Never place the center of interest in the middle of the painting. An off-center focal point is much more appealing to the eye. However, do not place it too close to an edge, which may lead the viewer's eye out of the painting.

1 Underpaint the Light Values
Watercolors change value with the addition of water or pigment. For this demonstration, think of value as ranging from 1 (light) to 9 (dark). Begin with no. 4 values. Underpaint the ears with Aureolin + Permanent Rose. Apply the cool grays with Ultramarine Blue + Permanent Rose + a touch of Aureolin to gray the mixture. Paint the tail and back by alternating with the cool gray mixture and the Aureolin + Permanent Rose mix. Paint the eyes with Aureolin + Ultramarine Blue. Paint the window area above the cat's back with Aureolin and Ultramarine Blue.

2 Darken the Values
Go back into the ears with Peach Black that is slightly darker than the underpainting. Then paint the head, shoulder area, tail and back with Peach Black, using more pigment and less water for a much darker value. On the face, chest and foot, apply a slightly darker value of the cool gray mix from step 1.

3 Paint the Window and Wall, Add Details
(See the completed painting on the opposite page.) Repaint the window, alternating between Aureolin and Ultramarine Blue. Paint the wall with a mix of Ultramarine Blue + Peach Black. Paint the sill with a no. 5 value mix of Permanent Rose + Ultramarine Blue + just a little Peach Black. Accent the eyes with more Peach Black. Add whiskers and highlight the closest eye with White Casein.

Himalayan Cat

PENNY SOTO

MEDIUM: *Acrylic ink & colored pencil*

COLORS: **FW Artists' Inks:** *Black • Raw Sienna • Cool Grey • Process Cyan • Flame Orange • Sepia • White • Yellow Ochre •* **Prismacolor Colored Pencils:** *dark brown • gray • purple*

BRUSHES: **Princeton:** *6300B square bristle bright no. 4 •* **Da Vinci:** *Top Acryl no. 8 •* **Iwata:** *airbrush*

OTHER SUPPLIES: *Crescent illustration board, 300 lb. (640gsm) • pencil • contact paper • craft knife*

1 Make a Drawing
Make a pencil drawing on illustration board. After checking the position, angles and measurements, shade in the darks and midtones, and save the white of the paper for the lights. Keep the drawing as simple as possible by sticking to these three values. Erase the graphite to leave a "ghost" of an image. Having the drawing and value plan in place will enable you to concentrate more on applying the colors.

2 Block In the Body
Using acrylic inks, start with your darkest colors first—in this case, Sepia. Block in the head, ears and paws and under the body. You can either paint wet-into-wet to achieve softer edges or use an airbrush as I did to speed things up. After the darks are blocked in, mix Raw Sienna + White + Yellow Ochre and block in the midtones, being careful not to paint over the saved lights. When this dries, apply a lighter value of the same three-color mix over the white of the paper. If you use an airbrush, protect the eyes and the background with contact paper cut to size for each area using a craft knife.

3 Lift Out Lighter Areas and Develop the Head
Start to lift out some of the fur in the lighter areas of the body with a no. 4 bright. There are hard edges all around the outside of the body; we'll soften them later.

Block in the eyes with Process Cyan. Work on the head next by mixing White + Sepia + a little Cool Grey and painting the fur in the midtone areas, using the no. 8 brush, following the direction of hair growth. Keep the face, nose, mouth and ears on the dark side for now; we'll build up these areas with lights later on.

artist's comment

My goal in this painting was to capture the likeness of my beloved Mendocino, whom we recently lost to cancer. The best way to do this is with careful observation of measurement, angles, form, color and value. If you study these aspects of your subject, you can achieve an exact likeness.

Himalayan Cat

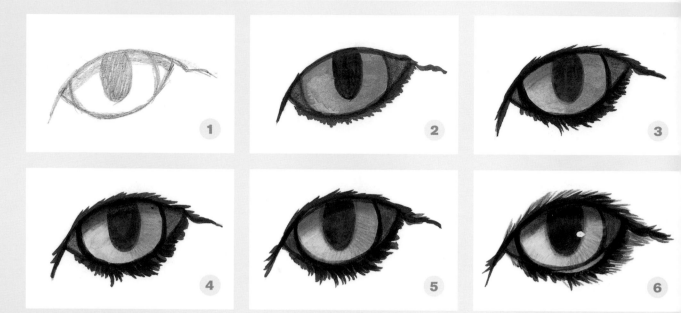

EYE DETAIL

1 Sketch the Eye
Sketch the eye in pencil, placing the three values: dark, mid-tone and the white of the paper for the light.

2 Paint the Iris, Pupil and Eye Corners
Paint the iris with Process Cyan, then the pupil and lids with Black. Use Sepia for the corners of the eye.

3 Soften the Edges and Add a Shadow
Using Black, soften the edges. Paint a Sepia shadow along the top of the iris, softening the edge.

4 Add the Reflection
Apply White on the left of the eye opposite the highlight (see step 6 for placement). This is the reflection of the highlight coming through the eye.

5 Soften
Paint Sepia around the pupil to soften it. Do the same along the bottom of the iris.

6 Add the Highlights
Use Sepia to soften the fur around the eye. Add the bright White highlight on the right side of the pupil. Water down the white and add some on the bottom lid.

4 Paint the Eyes, Light Fur and Paws

Paint the eyes following the instructions on page 12. Then paint the light fur on the body using White + Cool Grey + a bit of Sepia with the no. 8 brush. Keep it on the dark side to build up later. Use Sepia for the paws, painting in the direction of fur growth. Add highlights to the paws with Cool Grey.

Repeat the process, this time lightening the colors and working past the hard edges on the outside.

5 Finish the Fur and the Bar Stool

Block in the bar stool with a mix of Burnt Sienna + Sepia + Flame Orange, then lift out the highlights. When dry, use dark brown pencil to draw the wood grain.

Using Sepia + Raw Sienna for the darker fur and White + a bit of Raw Sienna for the lighter fur, work back and forth, adding color then blending and softening it. Adjust the highlights as needed. For colorful accents, add some different colors on top of the painting with both acrylic inks and colored pencils. Add purple pencil around the face and in the shadows under the body, some grays to the nose to bring it out a little more, Flame Orange on the bar stool and some Cool Grey on the bottom of the stool.

Longhaired Cat

LIAN QUAN ZHEN

MEDIUM: *Watercolor*

COLORS: **Van Gogh Water Colours:** *Azo Yellow Medium* • *Permanent Red Deep* • **Winsor & Newton Artists' Water Colour:** *Antwerp Blue*

BRUSHES: *Round no. 4 • flat ½-inch (13mm) • medium fan*

OTHER SUPPLIES: *Cold-pressed watercolor paper, 140 lb. (300gsm) • no. 2 pencil*

1 **2** **3**

4

5

1 Sketch and Splash
Sketch the cat lightly in pencil. Use the flat brush to splash a little water, yellow and red on the cat. It's OK to let some color run outside the boundaries of the image.

2 Blow
Put your mouth very close to the splashed area and blow the colors in different directions: toward the right for the tail, downward for the legs and radiating outward for the head.

3 Apply a Brown Mix
Mix yellow + red + a little blue to create a brown mix. While the colors on the painting are wet, apply the mix on the head, tail and legs using the flat brush. Let the colors blend.

4 Create Hair Texture
Using the fan brush and thick pigments, brush mix the three colors into a dark brown and paint the hair texture while the colors already on the cat are about 50-percent dry.

5 Continue the Hair and Begin the Face
Continue painting the hair texture, using a lighter brown on the face, back and upper body. Use a darker brown and a no. 4 round to paint the nose and around the eyes.

6 Finish the Face Details
(See the completed painting on the opposite page.) Mix blue + red (5:1) straight from the tubes. With this very dark bluish color and a no. 4 round, outline the eyes, nose and ears. For the eyeballs, apply yellow first, then glaze the upper parts with blue. Paint the pupils with a very dark brown.

Playful Kittens 1

SHERRY C. NELSON

MEDIUM: *Oil*

COLORS: **Winsor & Newton Artists' Oil Colours:** *Burnt Sienna • Charcoal Grey • Ivory Black • Raw Sienna • Raw Umber • Sap Green • Titanium White*

BRUSHES: **Winsor & Newton:** *Regency Gold Series 710 short bright nos. 0, 2, 4 & 8 • Series 740 liner no. 0*

OTHER SUPPLIES: *Odorless thinner • paper towels*

artist's comment

Paint the kittens in the following order: tail, body, facial features, then the rest of the head. Paint all the stages for each element before moving on to the next element. Begin painting each section of fur at its outer edge and gradually move inward as you complete each area. Be patient; many individual brushstrokes are required to produce realistic animal fur, which takes time and attention.

Basecoat All Areas

Use a no. 2 bright to paint the short fur, such as the legs and face, and a no. 4 bright to paint the longer fur, such as the body and tail.

Dark fur: Sparsely basecoat the dark fur areas using Charcoal Grey and the flat side of the brush (for smoother coverage). Apply paint following the fur's growth direction.

Light fur: Basecoat the light fur areas on both kittens using Titanium White + Raw Sienna and the flat side of the brush. Apply paint following the fur's growth direction in each area.

Eyes: Basecoat using a no. 0 bright and Sap Green. Outline using a no. 0 liner and Ivory Black.

Noses: Basecoat using a no. 0 bright and Burnt Sienna.

Ears: Basecoat the pink areas using a no. 2 bright and Burnt Sienna + Titanium White. Basecoat the gray areas using varying mixtures of Ivory Black + Raw Umber + Titanium White. Place

the lightest value at the edge of each ear. Use Ivory Black to place the darkest values inside the ears.

Rest of the head: Use a no. 2 bright to basecoat the dark fur areas with Charcoal Grey and the light fur areas with Titanium White + Raw Sienna. Soften the ears' edges into the surrounding values.

Playful Kittens 1

2 Add Shading

Use a no. 2 bright to paint the short fur, such as the legs and face, and a no. 4 bright to paint the longer fur, such as the body and tail.

Dark fur: Refer to the Shading Placement Charts on the opposite page and use Ivory Black and the chisel edge of the brush to create subtle shading (tabby markings) in the dark fur areas only.

Light fur: Refer to the Shading Placement Charts and use Raw Umber to shade the light fur areas only. Blend where the Raw Umber meets the basecoat using the brush's chisel edge and following the growth direction. Shade between the toes with Raw Umber.

Eyes: Highlight using a no. 0 bright and Sap Green + Titanium White + Raw Sienna. Use a no. 0 liner to add a dot of Titanium White.

Noses: Using a touch of Burnt Sienna + Titanium White and the tip of a no. 0 liner, stipple a highlight to create a little texture where the Burnt Sienna meets the fur.

Ears: Blend just a little where the values meet. You'll soften the ears when you paint the rest of the head.

Rest of the head: Using the same brush, shade the dark fur areas on each face with Ivory Black and the light fur areas with Raw Umber. Then add highlights to both with Titanium White. Use short strokes in this area to indicate shorter fur.

artist's comment

Connect areas of different colors and values with chisel strokes, lightly working the chisel edge of the brush on the line where the values meet. To avoid muddy color, apply paint sparingly, leaving some of the surface showing through.

artist's comment

To suggest dimension, each patch of fur must contain a range of values. On the kittens, you'll basecoat, shade and add highlights even in an area that appears completely black or white.

To apply shading and highlighting, make many overlapping strokes with the chisel edge of the brush. For a realistic look, always follow the growth direction of each patch of fur, layering hairs as you move from the tail toward the head.

Different areas of fur grow to different lengths, so adjust the lengths of your brushstrokes accordingly. The head and face often have shorter hairs; the chest, belly and tail have longer fur.

SHADING PLACEMENT CHARTS

Playful Kittens 1

3 Add Highlights and Whiskers

Use a no. 2 bright to paint the short fur, such as the legs and face, and a no. 4 bright to paint the longer fur, such as the body and tail.

Dark fur: Add highlights using the chisel edge of the "dirty" (uncleaned) brush and Titanium White. Don't overwork. Use light strokes to create a layered look.

Light fur: Add highlights using the chisel edge of the brush and Titanium White. Let dry and use the same color to reinforce highlights in the bright white areas.

Rest of the head: Highlight the whisker pads on each face using the same brush and Titanium White. Thin the same color with odorless thinner and use a no. 0 liner to add whiskers.

Dip a no. 8 bright into odorless thinner, then blot on a paper towel. Pull the brush along any rough edge to clean it up.

Playful Kitten 2

LIAN QUAN ZHEN

MEDIUM: *Chinese watercolor & ink*

COLORS: **Marie's Chinese painting colors or sumi colors:** *Phthalo Blue* • *Rouge* • *Vermilion* • *White* • **Chinese painting ink or sumi ink:** *Black*

BRUSHES: **Chinese brushes:** *small* • *medium* • *large*

OTHER SUPPLIES: *Raw Shuan paper (unsized rice paper), 12" × 15" (31cm × 38cm)*

Playful Kitten 2

1 Sketch With Ink
Lightly wet the small brush and load it with ink. Sketch the kitten, using light ink for the head, legs and body and darker ink for the eyes and ears. Move the brush quickly to avoid having too much ink blend on the paper.

2 Apply Three Strokes for the Body
Wet the large brush and load Phthalo Blue at the base, Rouge on the middle and dark ink on the tip (see Artist's Comment). Holding the brush sideways with the tip pointing to the left, apply three strokes from the shoulder to the hip and down to the thigh.

3 Add the Tail, Neck, Paws and Chest
Reload the large brush as you did in step 2. Hold it sideways to paint the tail in one stroke from the kitten's rear to the tail tip. Also paint the head in a few strokes with the brush tip pointing toward the eyes. Use the left-over color in the brush to paint the neck, paws and chest.

artist's comment

Here's how to load several colors on a Chinese brush:

1 Soak the brush in water and let the water drip from the tip. Holding the brush sideways, use the heel to pick up the first color, touching lightly. Roll the brush on the palette to allow all sides of the heel to absorb the color.
2 Use the brush middle to pick up the second color.
3 Dip the brush tip into the third color. Roll the brush lightly and then dab on the palette to let the colors blend smoothly.

4 Paint the Stripes
Load the medium brush with dark ink. Hold it straight up to paint the stripes when the previously applied colors are about 60-percent dry. Move the brush quickly to keep the ink from excessively blending into the colors.

5 Finish the Facial Details
Dip the small brush into Vermilion and Rouge. Highlight the tips of the ears and the right front paw. Then load with Phthalo Blue to paint the eyes, leaving highlights in the centers. Paint the pupils with dark ink. Finally, paint the whiskers and highlight the upper part of the eyes with thick White.

Sleepy Cat

GAYLE LAIBLE

MEDIUM: *Watercolor*

COLORS: **MaimeriBlu Watercolors:** *Dragon's Blood • Indian Yellow • Ultramarine Light •* **Orange Mix:** *Indian Yellow + Dragon's Blood •* **Dirty Purple Mix:** *Ultramarine Light + Dragon's Blood •* **Black Mix:** *Ultramarine Light + Dragon's Blood + a touch of Indian Yellow*

BRUSHES: **Royal & Langnickel:** *Series SG700 Soft Grip Golden Taklon glaze/wash ½-inch (13mm) • Series SG3000 Soft Grip Combo round nos. 6 & 10 • Series SG930 Soft Grip Golden Taklon filbert comb ¼-inch (6mm) • Series 6050 Nocturna script liner no. 1*

1 Sketch, Wash and Begin Shading

Sketch the cat. Use a ½-inch (13mm) glaze/wash brush to wash Orange Mix over the face, ears and patches—but not the white area. Let dry. Use a no. 10 round and the Dirty Purple Mix to shade between the closed eyes, down the nose and in the stripes above the nose and eyes. Soften out the edges. Using a no. 6 round, shade on the left and right side of the white stripe behind the head and on all shaded white areas.

2 Continue Shading, Wash In the Stripes

Use a no. 10 round and the Orange Mix + a touch of Ultramarine Light to shade behind the left ear and in front of both ears. Shade the top of the ears toward the front, leaving a fine light line, and where the ears attach to the head. Place a thin line of orange along the eyelids and across the nose tip. Wash in the stripes with a ½-inch (13mm) glaze/wash or a no. 10 round, softening the edges on both sides.

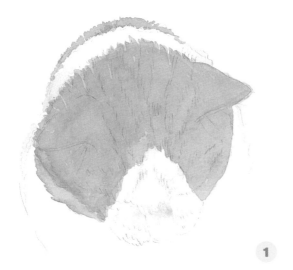

3 Create the Illusion of Fur

Darken the Orange Mix with a touch more Ultramarine Light and shade again with the same brush to build color. With the no. 6 round, pull little strokes through the stripes to create the look of hairs. Pull little strokes around the edges of the orange area for the illusion of fur. Also pull strokes from the ears. Darken the eyes and nose with a little Dirty Purple Mix. Wash a little orange across the nose bridge. Using a ¼-inch (6mm) filbert comb and the darkened Orange Mix, lightly stroke over the orange area, keeping the strokes lighter than the stripes. Lightly stroke the Dirty Purple Mix over the shaded area on the white, creating the illusion of fur.

4 Apply Finishing Touches

(See the completed painting on the opposite page.) Add a little more Ultramarine Light to the Orange Mix in step 3. Shade under the ears and where they attach to the head with a no. 10 round. Stroke in the stripes. Using a filbert comb, lightly stroke behind the left ear. Use the Dirty Purple Mix to stroke hair coming from the ears. Using a liner, dab a bit on the eyelids, stroke a line at the lower edge of the nose and dab dots from which the whiskers grow. Using thinned Black Mix and a liner, darken the eyelids and the edge of the nose. Lightly stroke in the whiskers with thinned Black or Dirty Purple Mix.

artist's comment

I saw this cat sitting and falling alseep in the sun and fell in love with him. The painting is a wonderful lesson in color mixing. Only red, blue and yellow are used.

Tabby Cat 1

JEANNE FILLER SCOTT

MEDIUM: *Acrylic*

COLORS: **Liquitex Artist Acrylics:** *Burnt Sienna • Burnt Umber • Cadmium Orange • Cadmium Red Light Hue • Cadmium Yellow Light • Payne's Gray • Raw Sienna • Titanium White • Ultramarine Blue*

BRUSHES: *Round nos. 1, 3, 4 & 8 • shader no. 10 (Brushes may be either sable or synthetic sable)*

OTHER SUPPLIES: *Gessobord • no. 2 pencil • kneaded eraser • jar of water • paper towels • palette knife (for mixing colors)*

1 Establish the Form

Draw the cat's head lightly in pencil, using a kneaded eraser to lighten any lines that are too dark. With a no. 4 round and Payne's Gray thinned with water, paint the main lines.

2 Paint the Dark Values

Start with the darkest color, which is Dark Mix. With a no. 4 round, paint the lines around the eyes, the pupils, the darker stripes and the shadowed areas. Use parallel brushstrokes that follow the fur pattern. Intensify the darkness around the eyes and the darker stripes by allowing the first layer of paint to dry and then applying a second coat.

3 Paint the Middle Values

With Warm Gray Mix and a no. 4 round, paint parallel strokes that overlap the edges of the adjoining Dark Mix. Switch to a no. 8 round for the broader areas. Use Dark Mix and a no. 4 round to reestablish any of the dark-value color that becomes obscured.

COLOR MIX FORMULAS

Dark: Burnt Umber + Ultramarine Blue
Warm Gray: Burnt Umber + Ultramarine Blue + Titanium White

Tabby Cat 1

4 Paint the Shadowed Fur, Begin the Eyes and Nose
Paint the shadowed parts of the muzzle, around the eyes, the base of the ears and other parts of the cat's coat with Bluish Shadow Mix and a no. 4 round. With a separate no. 4 round, blend the edges with the adjoining color, using small, parallel strokes.

Paint the nose with Nose Mix and a no. 4 round. Reestablish the nostrils with a no. 1 round and Dark Mix. Paint the eyes with Green Eye Mix. Reestablish the pupils with a no. 1 round and Dark Mix.

5 Paint the Background and Lighter Values, Begin Details
Paint over the green eye color and the dark lines around the eyes with thin Eye Glaze Mix.

Paint the area behind the cat with Background Mix and a no. 10 shader, using dabbing strokes. For the areas right next to the cat, use a no. 3 round.

Paint the light buff fur with Buff Mix and a no. 3 round, using strokes that follow the hair pattern. Overlap the edges of the surrounding color. Paint the inside of the ears with Pink Mix and a no. 3 round. With a separate no. 3 round and Dark Mix + a little Titanium White to lighten, paint fine parallel strokes along the ear edges into the pink. Paint the lightest areas of fur with Light Fur Mix and a no. 3 round.

COLOR MIX FORMULAS

Background: Titanium White + Ultramarine Blue + small amount of Burnt Sienna
Bluish Shadow: Titanium White + Ultramarine Blue + small amount of Burnt Umber
Buff: Titanium White + small amounts of Burnt Umber and Raw Sienna
Dark: Burnt Umber + Ultramarine Blue
Eye Glaze: Burnt Umber + Burnt Sienna + water
Eye Highlight: Titanium White + small amount of Ultramarine Blue
Green Eye: Cadmium Yellow Light + Burnt Umber + a touch of Cadmium Red Light Hue
Light Fur: Titanium White + small amount of Cadmium Yellow Light
Nose: Cadmium Red Light Hue + Titanium White + Burnt Umber
Pink: Titanium White + Cadmium Red Light Hue + Cadmium Orange + Burnt Sienna + Raw Sienna
Warm Gray: Burnt Umber + Ultramarine Blue + Titanium White

6 Refine and Add Detail

With a no. 3 round, add a glaze of Burnt Umber + water to the eyes. With the same brush, mix Green Eye Mix + Burnt Umber + a little Ultramarine Blue. Then use a dry brush to lightly dab this color into the eyes for shadow detail. Blend with a clean, moistened no. 3 round. With a semidry no. 3 round and Eye Highlight Mix, paint eye highlights with curving strokes.

Use Pink Mix + Burnt Sienna and a no. 3 round to paint some parallel strokes over the original pink in the ears, letting some of the original color show through.

Use a no. 1 round and Buff Mix to detail the dark areas of the fur. With a separate no. 1 round, blend and overlap some of the buff-colored areas with Warm Gray Mix. Use small, parallel strokes that follow the fur pattern.

Paint the highlighted edges of the ears and the ear tufts with a no. 1 round and Light Fur Mix.

Add another layer of Background Mix with a no. 10 shader.

7 Add Finishing Details

With a no. 1 round, continue to add dark fur detail with Dark Mix. Use a no. 3 round for the broader areas. If the detail needs to be a little lighter, add more water to your brush. Reestablish the pupils with Dark Mix and a no. 1 round. For shadows in the highlighted fur areas, use Warm Gray Mix + Titanium White and paint with a no. 3 round. Use a separate no. 3 round with Titanium White to blend the edges wet-into-wet and to soften the highlighted outline of the cat against the background. With a no. 3 round and Bluish Shadow mix, add color to the muzzle and reestablish lighter fur areas that have become obscured.

Use Dark Mix + Cadmium Red Light Hue and a no. 1 round to add shadow detail to the pink nose. Darken the shadow under the top eyelid with a no. 1 round and Dark Mix, using short vertical strokes from the top down.

Add depth to the background with two shaders. With the first, use Background Mix + bits of Ultramarine Blue and Burnt Umber and paint the darker color around the edges of the painting, working inward with semicircular strokes. With the second, use Background Mix and blend back into the darker color.

Paint the whiskers on the highlighted side of the face with a no. 1 round and Titanium White. Use Bluish Shadow Mix + Titanium White for the shadowed side. Dip your brush tip into the water and then into the paint. Use long, sweeping strokes. If necessary, tone them down with Warm Gray Mix.

Tabby Cat 2

LEE HAMMOND

MEDIUM: *Watercolor*

COLORS: *Cadmium Red Medium • Van Dyke Brown • Yellow Ochre (Color names may vary from brand to brand)*

BRUSHES: *Round nos. 1 & 2 • filbert no. 4 • detail no. 3/0 (Brushes may be either sable or synthetic)*

OTHER SUPPLIES: *Graphite pencil • kneaded eraser • ruler • craft knife • plastic palette • jar of water • watercolor paper • drawing board or smooth, rigid surface • masking or artist's tape (to affix watercolor paper to the board) • hair dryer or heat gun (optional)*

artist's comment

The grid technique allows you to capture an accurate line drawing from a photo. Simply reproduce the shapes in the photo grid squares into the corresponding grid squares on your watercolor paper. When you're sure of the accuracy of your drawing, erase the grid lines with a kneaded eraser.

1

2

1 Wash In the First Values
Add water to a well in your plastic palette. Take a small amount of Yellow Ochre with a no. 4 filbert and add it to the water. Wash both ears and down the front and sides of the face with this diluted color. Use the tip of a no. 1 round to add a small amount of Van Dyke Brown to the diluted Yellow Ochre and fill in the irises.

2 Wash In the Background and Continue the Cat
Create a diluted mixture of Van Dyke Brown + Yellow Ochre + Cadmium Red Medium. Wash this into the background with a no. 4 filbert, allowing it to become mottled and darker in the paper corners.

Add dark fur stripes with diluted Van Dyke Brown and a no. 2 round, following the patterns created in your drawing.

Intensify the eye with a deeper application of Yellow Ochre and a no. 1 round. Add some Cadmium Red Medium to the Yellow Ochre for the area around the pupil. Fill in the pupil with pure Van Dyke Brown and a 3/0 detail brush.

Wash diluted background colors into the cat's lower body.

3 Layer Colors and Add Whiskers
(See the completed painting on the opposite page.) Layer darker colors on top of the first washes. Because watercolors lighten as they dry, you may want to dry between layers with a hair dryer or heat gun to help you assess the values. Continue adding paint, increasing the amount of pigment in the mix. When you're finished layering and the painting is totally dry, add whiskers by quickly scraping them out with a sharp craft knife.

Tabby Cat 3

KAREN HUBBARD

MEDIUM: *Acrylic*

COLORS: **Delta Ceramcoat:** *Black • Butter Yellow • Gypsy Rose • Hippo Grey • Magnolia White • Mocha Brown • Old Parchment • Quaker Grey*

BRUSHES: *Round sable no. 4 (for the fur) • script liner no. 1 • flat ¾-inch (19mm) (Unless otherwise specified, use large brushes to paint large areas and smaller ones for small areas.)*

artist's comment

- The fur-stroke technique I refer to in the instructions is done with a flattened round sable brush, slightly thinned paint and short overlapping brushstrokes.
- For instructions on how to do the float technique referred to in some of the steps, see the Artist's Comment on page 7.

1 Start the Basecoat and Shadows
Basecoat the entire cat with Quaker Grey. Then basecoat the dark patches with Hippo Grey. Create shadows in the light gray areas with Hippo Grey fur strokes. Basecoat the nose, mouth and inside of the ears with Gypsy Rose.

2 Base the Eyes, Add Fur Strokes on Stripes
Basecoat the irises with Butter Yellow. Basecoat the pupils and the thin areas surrounding the irises with Black. Paint Black fur strokes on the dark patches, making the strokes denser for the stripes and softer and lighter for the shadows.

Tabby Cat 3

3 Shade

For body shading (inside the ears, under the mouth line, under the chin, around the muzzle, on the edges of the legs and between the toes), float with Hippo Grey. Float with transparent Black along the edge of the back, on the lower edge of the tail and on the belly. Shade across the upper edges of the irises with a float of Mocha Brown. Shade with Black around the nostrils and outer corners of the nose.

4 Highlight the Fur, Continue the Eyes

Highlight the dark fur patches between the stripes with fur strokes of Quaker Grey. Highlight all the light fur with fur strokes of Old Parchment. Shade around the pupils with a float of Black. When dry, float across the tops of the eyeballs with the same color. Float Black along the back edge of the cat and next to the hip.

5 Add Finishing Touches
Highlight the white fur with fur strokes of Magnolia White directly over the Old Parchment. Add a touch of Magnolia White on the tail and a tiny dab on the nose. Paint the whiskers with Magnolia White. Dampen the surface of the eyes and paint a reflected light of Hippo Grey + Quaker Grey (1:1) in the upper part of the eyes. Paint a tiny float of Old Parchment at the lower edge of the irises. Add a Magnolia White dot for sparkle.

Tuxedo Cat

Claudia Nice

MEDIUM: *Watercolor with pen & ink*

COLORS: **M. Graham & Company Watercolor:** *Burnt Sienna • Cobalt Blue • Dioxazine Purple • Hooker's Green • Ivory Black or Lamp Black • Yellow Ochre*

BRUSHES: *Flat stroke ¼-inch (6mm) • round sable no. 4 • round detail sable no. 00 (Unless otherwise specified, use large brushes to paint large areas and smaller ones for small areas.)*

OTHER SUPPLIES: *Cold-pressed watercolor paper, 8" × 10" (20cm × 25cm) • Masquepen • Rapidograph .25mm pen & black India ink or a Pigma Micron pen no. 005 • facial tissue • pencil masking tape*

1 Sketch the Face

2

3

4

1 Sketch the Face

Sketch the face in pencil. The blue lines are a visual guide showing the direction the hair grows.

2 Begin Eye, Apply Masking, Base Wash the Pink Areas

Begin painting the eye as shown in the Eye Detail instructions (page 38). Mask out the hairs and whiskers shown in blue, using a Masquepen. Base wash the pink areas, using a no. 4 round and a pale rose wash muted with Burnt Sienna.

3 Base Wash the White Areas, Shade the Nose and Ears

Lay down the base wash in the shadow areas of the white hair following the Fur Detail instructions (pages 38-39). Shade the darker areas of the nose and ears with a second layer of the pink mix from step 2.

4 Add Hair Texture

Add hair strokes over the white shadow areas. Stroke penwork into the black hair areas, paying close attention to the hair growth direction shown in step 1. For more specific instruction on developing the black hair, see Fur Detail on pages 38-39. (General painting instructions continue on page 39.)

artist's comment

On this page and the bottom of page 39 are general painting directions. The following two pages give detailed instructions for painting the upward gazing eye and the fur.

Tuxedo Cat

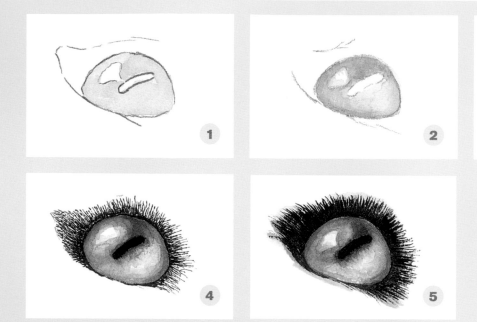

EYE DETAIL

1 Sketch the Eye, Basecoat the Iris
Sketch the eye lightly in pencil, indicating the pupil and light reflection areas. Basecoat the iris with a pale wash of Yellow Ochre muted with a touch of Dioxazine Purple, leaving the reflection area white. Let dry.

2 Add Darks to the Iris, Wash the Reflection Spot
Darken the area above the pupil and around the edge of the eye with a second Yellow Ochre + Dioxazine Purple wash. Soften the inner edges with a clean, damp brush. Let dry. Paint the bottom of the reflection spot with an extremely pale Cobalt Blue wash, grayed with a hint of black.

3 Add Green Around the Pupil, Darken the Outer Eye Edge
Dampen the area around the pupil and use a no. 00 round to touch a mixture of Hooker's Green muted with Burnt Sienna to the pencil outline of the pupil. Allow the green to bleed into the damp area, forming "rays." If it flows too far, blot it with a tissue. Apply a little green from the pupil to the top of the eye. Let dry. Blend a little Burnt Sienna around the outer edge of the eye.

4 Outline the Eye, Radiate Hair
Use the pen to outline the eye and stroke in hair texture lines radiating outward from the eye.

5 Apply a Black Wash
Paint a wash of black over the ink lines.

FUR DETAIL

1 Ink Individual Hairs
Draw individual hairs in the black sections with the pen. Use a crisscross stroke with the lines no longer than the actual hairs would be. Stroke the pen in the direction the hairs would lie.

2 Overlap Edges
Let the lines at the black fur edges overlap into the white areas or off the edge of the cat. Don't make a solid outline.

3 Apply a Black Wash
Paint the black fur area with a wash of black watercolor, using a no. 4 round. Make the wash dark enough to look black but not so heavy as to cover all the ink lines. Use a no. 00 round to help blend the inkwork and paint strokes at the edges.

4 Basecoat the Shadowed White Fur
Leave white highlighted fur areas unpainted. Basecoat shadow areas with a very pale (off-white) mix of Yellow Ochre muted with a touch of Dioxazine Purple. Apply this mix to a damp surface with a no. 4 round. Add a little more of the purple to the mix for the deepest shadow areas. Let the wash dry completely.

5 Begin the White Hair Strokes

Using a no. 00 round and the pale Yellow Ochre + Dioxazine Purple mix, apply crisscross hair strokes over the areas of off-white wash. Stroke in the direction that the hair grows.

6 Stroke In the Shadowed White Fur

Stroke hair lines into the deep shadow areas, using the mix from step 5 with slightly more purple added.

(General painting instructions continued from page 37)

5 Add the Background and Refine the Whiskers

After finishing the fur, dampen the background area of the paper. Dab varied mixes of Hooker's Green + black onto the background and let it flow. The darkest wash should be in the area of the white muzzle for contrast. Use the stroke brush and work quickly. Soften the outer edges by blotting them with a facial tissue.

Remove the masking by dabbing it with masking tape, sticky side down. Narrow the whiskers with pen or paint as needed.

Dogs

Man's best friend comes in countless shapes and sizes, and characteristics can vary slightly or widely from breed to breed. In this section are some of the better-known varieties, from purebreds to mutts. Study the pets you want to portray, learning what qualities make them unique. Look too for common threads among them to discover which techniques will work for multiple breeds.

Australian Shepherd

ERIN O'TOOLE

MEDIUM: *Watercolor & gouache*

COLORS: **Holbein Artists' Watercolors:** *Burnt Sienna • Cobalt Blue • Peach Black •* **Winsor & Newton Designers Gouache:** *Permanent White • Raw Sienna*

BRUSHES: **Isabey:** *kolinsky sable no. 6 •* **Winsor & Newton:** *University Series 233 short handled round no. 1 •* **Generic:** *old paintbrush (Unless otherwise specified, use large brushes to paint large areas and smaller brushes for small ones.)*

OTHER SUPPLIES: *Nideggan paper • Dr. Ph. Martin's Bleed Proof White • General's charcoal pencil (HB hard) • Blair Very Low Odor Spray Fixative*

1 Transfer the Sketch and Begin the Darks and Lights

Using simple pencil lines, copy the reference sketch in larger form to a bigger sheet of paper. Paint the darkest shadows and an indication of the collar with Peach Black using the no. 6 sable. Indicate the shadow side of the dog with a pale wash of the same color. Use bleedproof white for the white highlights on the back, head, ruff and legs. Mix Raw Sienna + Burnt Sienna for the copper-colored eyebrows and upper legs.

2 Develop the Shadow Side

With a cool blue-gray mix of Permanent White + Cobalt Blue + Peach Black, paint the shadow side of the ruff, body, legs and muzzle. Add more or less white to vary the mixture, working from lighter to darker as you head toward the rear of the dog. Add the dog tag with the same mix.

3 Finish the Details and the Hair

(See the completed painting on the opposite page.) Paint the pupil and the eyelids with Peach Black. Put an undercoat of Permanent White on the iris; when it dries, paint over it with Cobalt Blue. Hardly any of the white of the eye shows on dogs. Use bleedproof white for the highlights on both eyes.

  Using the same blue-gray mix from step 2, paint the grayish markings around the eye, on the ear and down the neck. A light, loose stroke brings life to the painting. Use a little Burnt Sienna in the mouth.

  Carefully give detail to the legs. The area from the elbow to the wrist is thin, so paint it with swift, straight strokes. The wrist is round, and the turn of the nails shows the position of the foot.

  Paint the longer hairs of the dog with a thin mix of Peach Black + the blue-gray mix from step 2. You can splay the hairs of an old paintbrush to use just for this purpose. Bring out of the white hairs on the light side of the dog with small strokes of bleedproof white. Lightly detail the collar and dog tag with Burnt Sienna.

artist's comment

The light was shining brightly on one side of my dog when I did this quick reference sketch. I worked quickly, using a charcoal pencil in my tiny field journal. I added white and other colors later to show where her white fur picked up the light.

Basset Hound

PAT WEAVER

MEDIUM: *Watercolor*

COLORS: **Da Vinci:** *Burnt Sienna* • *Ultramarine Blue* • **Daniel Smith:** *Quinacridone Gold* •
Shiva Casein: *Titanium White*

BRUSHES: **Loew-Cornell:** *Series 7020 Golden Taklon Ultra round nos. 10 & 14* • *Series 7700 Golden Taklon
"Grande" round wash no. 30 (Unless otherwise specified, use large brushes to paint large areas
and smaller brushes for small ones.)*

OTHER SUPPLIES: *Cold-pressed watercolor paper, 140 lb. (300gsm)*

artist's comment

American Kennel Club dog shows provide a wealth of painting material. That is where I found this basset hound entering the ring for judging.

1 Apply the Underpainting
Underpaint the basset hound, alternating between Burnt Sienna and Quinacridone Gold in the warm areas and a mix of Ultramarine Blue + a little Burnt Sienna for the cool gray areas.

2 Add Darks and Accents to the Face
Apply a darker value of the Ultramarine Blue + Burnt Sienna mix to the dog's ears and face. Accent the eyes with more of the same mix, maintaining some of the original underpainting at the same time. Paint the nose using Ultramarine Blue + Burnt Sienna, darkening the value just a little in the gray areas. Add the shadow under the dog with alternating applications of Ultramarine Blue, Burnt Sienna and a little Quinacridone Gold.

3 Punch Up the Darks and Add Highlights and a Background
(See the completed painting on the opposite page.) Accent the darks in the ears more using Ultramarine Blue + Burnt Sienna. Also add more accenting in the shadow under the dog. Add the eye highlight with White Casein and the nose highlight with White Casein + a little Ultramarine Blue + Burnt Sienna mix.

Paint the background with a thin gray mix of Ultramarine Blue + Burnt Sienna + a little Quinacridone Gold + a lot of water. Be sure that the background is the correct value against the dog and the tail. If you make it too dark, you will lose the impact of the dog; if it's too light, you'll lose the tail and the top of the head.

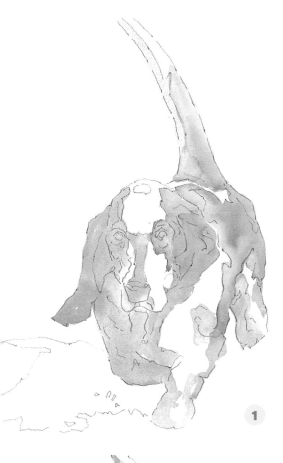

1

2

Border Collie

MAUREEN SHIER

MEDIUM: *Resin acrylic*

COLORS: **JansenArt Traditions:** *Blue Grey • Brown Madder • Burgundy • Burnt Sienna • Burnt Umber • Carbon Black • Dark Grey • Light Grey • Medium Beige • Medium Grey • Medium White • Titanium White • Ultramarine Blue • Warm White • Yellow Oxide*

BRUSHES: **Scharff:** *Series 100 Classic bright nos. 2, 6, 10 & 14 • Series 140 Golden Taklon flat nos. 12 & 16 • Series 405 Golden Taklon round no. 3 • Series 407 Red Sable round no. 5 • Series 480 Golden Taklon scroller no. 0 (Unless otherwise specified, use large brushes to paint large areas and smaller brushes for small ones.)*

OTHER SUPPLIES: *Museum board, 10" x 12" (25cm x 30cm) • JansenArt Glazing Medium • white chalk pencil (optional) • Masterson Sta-Wet Palette*

1 Block In

(Refer to the Color Mix Formulas on page 46 for all steps on this page.) Base in an opaque background with Mix 10, adding some glazing medium to the paint to promote smooth coverage. Apply a coat of glazing medium and let it dry.

Block in the first layer of paint. Block in the mouth with Mixes 1, 3, 4 and 5, noting the different values of red. Block in the teeth with Medium White + Titanium White (1:1). For the eye, block in the iris with Mix 8 and the pupil with Carbon Black. Block in the dark fur with Mix 7 and the light fur with the Mix 6. Cover the entire painted area with a coat of glazing medium. (Fur and nose instruction continues on page 47; specific eye and mouth instruction continues on this page and on page 46.)

DEVELOP THE EYE

2 Shape the Eye

Begin to shape the eyeball, shading the iris with Burnt Sienna first. When this has dried, apply Burnt Umber over the same area but not as far out as the Burnt Sienna. Soften the pupil hue into the iris with Carbon Black.

3 Add Eyelids and Form

Shape the eyelids with Mixes 9A, 9B and 9C using a drybrush technique. Paint the outside corner of the eye with a brush mix of Mixes 1 and 9A. Blend out the intensity toward the outer edge where it meets the iris with Carbon Black. Use the same color to create the shadow on the iris that the top eyelid casts. Repeat these steps for the inside corner of the eye, this time with a brush mix of Mixes 3 and 9B. *Tip:* When drybrushing narrow areas, use the chisel edge of a small classic bright brush.

4 Finish With Detail

Add more intense color to the iris with a brush mix of Yellow Oxide and Titanium White, keeping this sparkle to the bottom between about 9 and 4 o'clock. Drybrush Mix 9C across the top of the pupil and iris without extending the line toward either outside edge. Using Titanium White, add the large highlight dot and touches of moisture where the eye meets the eyelid, where the highlight is the most intense. Use Mix 9C for less intense touches near the outside corner.

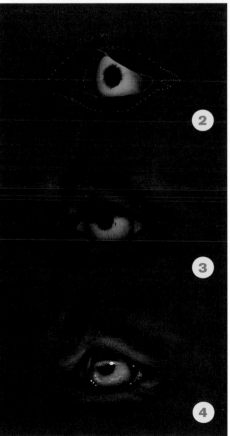

artist's comment

Apply a coat of glazing medium after you have completed an area on your painting. This not only helps to build depth in the painting, it also protects the acrylics you have applied.

Border Collie

DEVELOP THE MOUTH

2 Darken the Gums and Add Shadows

Darken and unify the gums by adding Mix 2, while allowing hints of the blocked-in color to remain. Blend this dark color up from fur area and down from the edge that meets the tongue. Drybrush Mix 9B on the tongue at its center and near the roof of the mouth. Deepen the tongue area at the corner of the mouth with Mix 2. Use the same color to glaze a large shadow across the tongue as well as the shadows that the foreground teeth create.

3 Develop the Gums

The moist area of the gums reflects some of the gum color. To portray these light areas, drybrush using the chisel edge of your classic bright and a brush mix of some of the blues and pinks on your palette. To create the illusion of moisture on these areas, apply dots and drags of the same blues and pinks directly over the drybrushed areas.

4 Finish the Teeth and Indicate Moisture

Block in the teeth again with Medium White + Titanium White (1:1) and, while still wet, add some Warm White to the light areas. Wipe the brush and add some of Mix 9C for the shaded areas. Keep the paint thick when applying, as this helps to create texture on the teeth. Don't allow the teeth to become too bright.

For the most intense moist areas of the mouth, apply Titanium White. Drybrush mix 9B on the tongue to further deepen it, then drybrush Titanium White to establish the highlight on the roll of the tongue.

COLOR MIX FORMULAS

Mix 1: Warm White + Burgundy + Medium White (3:1:1, light value 9)

Mix 2: Brown Madder + Burgundy + Burnt Umber + Medium Beige + Carbon Black (2:2:1:1:just a touch, dark value 2)

Mix 3: Mix 2 + touch of Burgundy (dark value 4)

Mix 4: Mix 3 + touch of Carbon Black (dark value 1)

Mix 5: Mix 3 + touch of Carbon Black (dark value 3)

Mix 6: Titanium White + Light Grey (5:1, light value 9)

Mix 7: Dark Grey + Carbon Black (3:1, dark value 2)

Mix 8: Yellow Oxide + Medium White (2:1, light value 7)

Mix 9A: Blue Grey + Medium Grey + Ultramarine Blue (2:2:1, midtone value 5)

Mix 9B: Mix 9A + Titanium White (light value 7)

Mix 9C: Mix 9B + Titanium White (light value 9)

Mix 10: Warm White + Medium White + Burnt Sienna (4:2:1, light value 9)

DEVELOP THE NOSE

2 Shape the Nostril and Create Form

The opening of a nostril is very wide, but place the values carefully so you don't make the nostril look pig-like. Shape the nose with Mix 9B, drybrushing for the first overall coverage of the nose area. Don't worry about covering too much of the nostril area, as a darker value will be added later to further define the opening. To add the lighter areas of the nose, drybrush with Mix 9C and a little Titanium White using a small bright brush. Add a touch of Mix 1 to the dirty brush and add a hint of skin-tone color to the inside top of the nostril as well as a chisel line of the nostril edge. Use a clean brush with Carbon Black to add the dark areas. The front of the nose is the darkest.

3 Add Details

Blend Carbon Black into the white fur on the bridge of the nose to soften the harsh line where the two colors meet. Blend together the remaining areas where these two colors meet. Drybrush Mix 9C below the nose and on the chin as well. Side-load a small flat and chop in Mix 6 for some intense coverage. Using the tip of a scroller brush over a surface dampened with equal parts glazing medium and water, add texture to the nose with dots of Mix 9C as well as some dots using a brush-mix of Titanium White and Mix 1. Apply more intense coverage to the light area under the nose with the flat brush side-loaded with Mix 6, then further brightened with Titanium White.

DEVELOP THE FUR

2 Build the Fur

"Landmark" some areas with a white chalk pencil to help in building the shape of the facial features and fur direction. Next, drybrush a small area of pink, identifying the area of the ear, using Mix 2. Then drybrush all of the under-fur using various brights. Use the flat of the brush for the larger areas or smooth areas of coverage; use the chisel of the brush for the narrow lines such as the strings of fur coming out from the ear. Apply the first overall coverage using Mix 9A, then apply Mixes 9B and 9C for the lighter areas and to shape the contours of the face and folds of the fur. Continue building shape by adding the darks where the areas recede, and use Carbon Black to deepen some areas that were lightened too much. Apply a coat of glazing medium after every value and hue is added to build depth in the fur.

3 Detail the Fur

Add fine lines indicating individual hairs as well as some texture that can be seen in the fur on the snout area. Dampen the short-hair area first with equal parts water and glazing medium. Then, with a fanned-out no. 5 red sable round loaded with Mix 9A, apply the texture with a tapping motion, using just the tips of the hairs on the brush. The moisture applied first allows the paint to "melt" into the background and, as it dries, allows more intense, smaller dots of color on top of this.

For the finer lines of individual fur, start with Mix 9C, progressing to a mix of this and Titanium White. Apply more detailed, controlled highlights using a scroller brush with the same blue values and finally Titanium White.

Boston Bull Terrier Puppy

PAT WEAVER

MEDIUM: *Watercolor*

COLORS: **Da Vinci:** *Burnt Sienna • Permanent Rose •* **Holbein:** *Peach Black •*
Winsor & Newton: *Quinacridone Gold*

BRUSHES: **Loew-Cornell:** *Series 7020 Golden Taklon Ultra round nos. 10 & 12 (Unless otherwise specified, use large brushes to paint large areas and smaller brushes for small ones.)*

OTHER SUPPLIES: *Cold-pressed watercolor paper, 140 lb. (300gsm) • White Casein*

artist's comment

When traveling around the country teaching workshops, I'm always looking for subjects to paint. I encountered this wonderful dog in Richmond, Virginia, outside a restaurant. Always keep that camera with you. You never know what's just around the corner.

1 Underpaint the Features
Underpaint the ears with Burnt Sienna and Permanent Rose. Paint the area beneath the nose with the same colors. Underpaint the eyes with Quinacridone Gold and Burnt Sienna. The gray is just Peach Black with a lot of water added. The value of each color should range from 4-5 (midtone).

2 Add Darks and Accents to the Face
Build up the face and ears with Peach Black, still keeping the value no darker than a 5, except for the lower portion of the lip, which will be slightly lighter. Be sure to preserve the white of the paper on the dog's face, shoulders and chest.

Paint the nose and accent the eyes with a mixture of Peach Black + Burnt Sienna. The collar is Permanent Rose accented with Permanent Rose + Peach Black.

3 Deepen the Values to Finish
Repaint the dog's head down into the shoulders with a 9 value of Peach Black and enough water so that the paint flows onto the paper. Leave a suggestion of pink in the ears. Accent the dark gray areas on the face and chest with a 6 value of Peach Black (more water added). Highlight the eyes with White Casein. Add a little Peach Black for the right eye highlight. Try to make the temperature of each highlight different—one warm and one cool but of the same value.

With a toothbrush dipped in water and blotted on a paper towel, lightly scrub the edges of the ears and shoulders straddling the paint and the white of the paper.

Boxer

BONNIE FREDERICO

MEDIUM: *Watercolor*

COLORS: ***Winsor & Newton:*** *Burnt Sienna • Burnt Umber • Gold Ochre • Ivory Black • Payne's Gray • Winsor Red*

BRUSHES: ***Royal:*** *Majestic round nos. 4, 6 & 5/0 (Unless otherwise specified, use large brushes to paint large areas and smaller brushes for small ones.)*

OTHER SUPPLIES: *Craft knife (optional)*

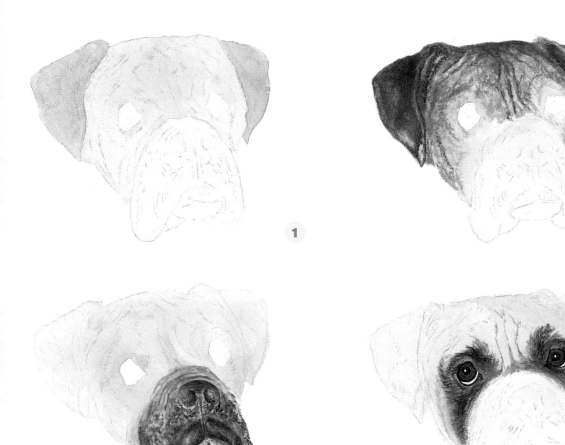

1 Apply the First Washes

Apply a wash to the face and the ears with a light value of Burnt Sienna + Burnt Umber. Paint a light-value wash of Ivory Black on the muzzle. Apply a wash to the chin area using Winsor Red and dirty water.

2 Drybrush Color Onto the Face

Using a drybrush technique, work the Burnt Sienna + Burnt Umber mix, Burnt Sienna, Burnt Umber and Ivory Black on the face and the ears. Make sure the color is applied in the direction of hair growth. Work small areas at a time, and add a wash of Gold Ochre as needed.

3 Develop the Mouth Area

Paint the muzzle and mouth area using Ivory Black + small amounts of Payne's Gray. Add washes to these areas, building values to form wrinkles and leathery jowls. Use the tip of your brush to form nostrils and hair follicles. Drybrush to give a mottled effect.

4 Finish the Eyes and the Surrounding Fur

Paint the iris with Burnt Umber. When this dries, add a black pupil. Try to leave a highlight; if this doesn't work, scratch out highlights later with a craft knife. Using Ivory Black, outline the rim of the iris and add the outline of the eye socket. Start forming the fur around the eye with a light value of black to establish the fur pattern. Darken the value as you add more layers for realism. Let some of the brown show through, or add it as needed.

artist's comment

Every dog has different colors and unique markings. Don't be bound by the colors I've chosen here; getting the values correct is more important.

Bulldog 1
PAT WEAVER

MEDIUM: *Watercolor & watercolor pencil*

COLORS: **Da Vinci:** *Ultramarine Blue* • **Holbein Artists' Watercolors:** *Aureolin* • *Burnt Sienna* • *Peach Black* • *Permanent Rose* • **Shiva Casein:** *Titanium White* • **Cretacolor Aqua Monolith watercolor pencils:** *Prussian Blue* • *Pompeian Red* • *Grass Green* • *Orange*

BRUSHES: **Loew-Cornell:** *Series 7020 Golden Taklon Ultra round nos. 10 & 14* • *Series 7700 Golden Taklon "Grande" round no. 30 (Unless otherwise specified, use large brushes to paint large areas and smaller brushes for small ones.)*

OTHER SUPPLIES: *Cold-pressed watercolor paper, 140 lb. (300gsm)*

1 Pencil the Dog
Draw the dog with watercolor pencils, alternating between blue, red, green and orange. This is a fun way to draw and also embellishes the painting.

2 Add Water and Underpaint the Features
Using clean water and a no. 10 round, wet the pencil drawing, pulling the color out onto the white of the paper. You will see how the pencil color melts as the water touches it.

Underpaint the eyes with Burnt Sienna. Paint the iris and accent the eyes with Peach Black. Paint the nose with a mix of Peach Black + Burnt Sienna. Underpaint the tongue with Burnt Sienna + Permanent Rose. Paint the areas inside the ears with a no. 4 value (midtone) of Burnt Sienna.

3 Develop the Features and Add the Remaining Accents
(See the completed painting on the opposite page.) Go back into the ears with a slightly darker mix of Burnt Sienna + Ultramarine Blue. Accent the inside of the ears with Peach Black.

Bring out the eyes more with Peach Black, and highlight with White Casein. Apply Permanent Rose for the little red area under the right eye. Paint the tongue darker with Permanent Rose + Burnt Sienna, and near the back of the mouth with Permanent Rose + Peach Black. Repaint the nose darker with Peach Black. Paint the collar with a mix of Permanent Rose + Aureolin. The darker red mix is Permanent Rose + Peach Black. Accent under the tongue with more Peach Black and Burnt Sienna. Paint the gray on the face and shoulders with a mix of Ultramarine Blue + Burnt Sienna.

Paint the background with a layer of Peach Black. Let this dry, then go back into it again, producing a very dark no. 9 value.

artist's comment

Drawing with watercolor pencils dipped in water provides some hard lines and soft lines all at the same time. Changing colors as you go adds a little interest to the image because you can still see the original watercolor pencil drawing even after the painting is finished. Making the drawing with watercolor pencil instead of graphite offers a fresh approach that enhances the white of the paper.

Bulldog 2

PEGGY HARRIS

MEDIUM: *Oil*

COLORS: **Martin/F. Weber Professional Permalba Oil Colors:** *Burnt Sienna • Burnt Umber • Cadmium Yellow Light • Ivory Black • Original Permalba White • Raw Umber • Vermilion Permanent •* **Fawn Mix:** *Cadmium Yellow Light + Raw Umber + a touch of Burnt Sienna*

BRUSHES: **Silver Brush, Ltd.:** *Series 2000S Golden Natural round no. 5/0 • Series 2008S Golden Natural square wash 1-inch (25mm) • Series 2502S Ruby Satin brights (stiff shaders) nos. 4 & 8 • Series 1000S Grand Prix white bristle round no. 4 • Series 2528S Ruby Satin filbert grass comb ¼-inch (6mm) • Series 2431S Ultra Mini designer round no. 2 • Series 5319S Wee Mops ⅛-inch (3mm), 3/16-inch (5mm), ¼-inch (6mm) & ⅜-inch (5mm) • Series 5519S Silver white oval mop ½-inch (13mm)*

OTHER SUPPLIES: *Res-N-Gel Oil Painting Medium • cotton swabs • odorless paint thinner • paper towels varnish or matte acrylic sealer*

1

2

1 Establish the Basic Wrinkle Pattern

With a no. 5/0 round, establish the eyes with Burnt Sienna and Ivory Black, the nose crease and jowl line with Ivory Black, and the nose and lip with Raw Umber.

Spread a slick of gel medium over the entire image with the wash brush. Using tiny mop brushes of appropriate size for each space, gently tap the Fawn Mix into predominant shadow areas and along major wrinkle lines. Wipe the brush clean and blend the color into the surrounding area.

2 Enhance and Blend the Colors

Intensify the fur color with tiny mop brushes and more Fawn Mix. Enhance the deepest shadows with Raw Umber. Once the paint is applied, wipe the mop clean and continue to blend the color. Stroke the mop in the direction of the fur growth. Occasionally reverse the stroke to prevent a buildup of paint along a line. Once rich color levels are achieved, lightly dust the entire image with a large, very soft oval mop. This will soften wrinkle lines and spread transparent color over the entire image without destroying the basic pattern.

artist's comment

Effortlessly create the myriad values seen in wrinkled fur with this oil lift-out technique using gel medium, cotton swabs and specialty brushes. This method is dependent upon paint being removed to reveal the background color for the highlights. For that reason, it is imperative to work on a white or light cream undercoat. Apply a light coat of varnish or matte acrylic sealer to the underpainting before painting the image. The slick surface will facilitate the lifting out of paint and promote more delicate hair lines.

This is a very fluid technique that allows you to repeat steps as many times as needed. Shadows and highlights almost magically develop as you work. Be prepared to take advantage of "happy accidents."

Bulldog 2

3

4

3 Lift Out and Reblend the Highlights

Lift out major highlights with cotton swabs. Reblend the highlights into the surrounding fur with small mop brushes. For the smoothest color transitions, frequently wipe the mop clean as you work. Repeat this step as often as needed to create glowing highlights. Proceed to create lesser highlight shapes. The smallest shapes may be lifted out with a stiff bright brush that has been dipped in thinner. Highlight centers may be further brightened with a cotton swab that has been dipped in thinner and then briefly blotted on a towel. Establish basic muzzle and chin markings with Ivory Black and a ⅛-inch (3mm) mop.

4 Perfect the Fur and Add Details

Add gel to areas where individual hair marks need more visibility. Stroke a clean filbert comb in an area to create even more hair marks. Extend light fur tips into dark shadows with a clean bristle brush, wiping the brush clean after each stroke. Perfect the muzzle and chin markings. Lightly dust the entire image with the large, soft oval mop.
Repaint the nose and lip with brush-mixed Ivory Black + Permalba White. Tint the lip with a touch of Vermilion. Refine the nostrils and mouth with thinned Ivory Black and a no. 5/0 round. Finish the eyes with Cadmium Yellow Light reflections and Permalba White highlights.

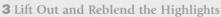

artist's comment

Keep in mind that the amount of gel medium used, either under or in the paint, controls not only the transparency of the paint, but also the quality of the fur portrayed. More gel and paint creates coarser, stiffer fur. Less gel and paint creates finer, softer fur.

Different brushes also contribute to the quality of the fur. Hog bristle brushes create stiff fur and have the greatest lift-out capacity. Filbert combs have little lift-out capability, but create very fine hair. Mops create the softest fur with a slightly fuzzed quality.

5

5 Adjust the Hues and Values With Glazes

Once the painting is dry, use your bright and square wash brushes to apply glazes of gel medium + color. If needed, use mops of appropriate size to dust out brush marks or blend the color into surrounding fur. Because the glazes are transparent, underlying fur marks will remain visible. Here, large areas were toned with gel medium + Fawn Color Mix. Small shadows were deepened with gel medium + Raw Umber or Burnt Umber. The tonality of the coat was changed with gel medium + Burnt Sienna. This is also an easy and effective way to add spots, stripes or other markings to animal fur.

German Shepherd

SHARRON ENGLAND

MEDIUM: *Oil*

COLORS: *Black • Burnt Sienna • Burnt Umber • Cadmium Orange • Cadmium Yellow Medium • Naples Yellow • Raw Sienna • Titanium White (Color names may vary from brand to brand)*

BRUSHES: **Royal:** *Golden Taklon filbert comb or wisp ¼-inch (6mm) & ½-inch (13mm) & filbert wisp ⅜-inch (5mm) • Series 5020 shader nos. 2, 4 & 8 • Series 2659 filbert no. 4 or Series 2719 mop ½-inch (13mm) • Series 2691 short liner no. 2 (Unless otherwise specified, use large brushes to paint large areas and smaller brushes for small ones.)*

OTHER SUPPLIES: *Res-N-Gel Oil Painting Medium*

1 Apply the Pattern

Transfer this pattern onto your painting surface.

2 Paint the Eyes and Nose, Then the Fur

When painting an animal, always start with the eyes. This gives the animal its personality and helps you paint the rest of the creature. Paint the nose next. See pages 60-61 for step-by-step instruction on painting these areas.

Next, following the value placement chart and Color Mix Formulas, block in the colors to establish the dog's form. Start with the light colors first (L), then the dark (D) and finish with the medium (M). Block this in very rough with uneven edges to make color-blending easier. Soften the edges of the colors with the chisel edge of a no. 4 and a no. 8 shader. (General painting instructions continue on page 61. The following two pages give detailed instructions for painting the eyes and nose.)

COLOR MIX FORMULAS

INSIDE EAR

Light: Burnt Sienna + Titanium White + pin drop of Burnt Umber
Medium: Burnt Sienna + Burnt Umber
Dark: Black

FUR

Light: Naples Yellow
Medium: Raw Sienna + Naples Yellow
Dark: Raw Sienna

MUZZLE

Light: Titanium White + Black (medium gray)
Medium: Light mix + Black + Burnt Umber
Dark: Medium mix + Black

German Shepherd

EYE DETAIL

1 Basecoat and Shade

Base paint the eye with Burnt Sienna. Looking at the eye as a clock (see Artist's Comment), shade from 9 to 3 o'clock with Burnt Umber. Outline the iris with Black, lightly pulling toward the center. Base paint the pupil with Black. Soften all edges.

2 Begin Iris Highlight

Highlight with Cadmium Orange from 3 to 6 o'clock, then soften the edges. Highlight from 4 to 5 o'clock with Cadmium Yellow Medium. On top of the orange, soften and reinforce with Cadmium Yellow Medium + Titanium White.

3 Blend and Add Details

Outline the lower lid with medium gray (Black + Titanium White), and highlight it with lighter gray. Paint the tear ducts with Burnt Sienna + Titanium White, and highlight them with a lighter version of the same mix. Add a sharp white highlight at 10 o'clock on the pupil.

artist's comment

Eyes are not hard to paint if you think of a clock while painting them.

1 Base paint the iris with a medium value of your color choice.
2 Shade from 9 to 3 o'clock with a dark value. Blend across the colors to soften.
3 Paint a light value from 3 to 6 o'clock and blend across.
4 Highlight on top of the light value from 4 to 5 o'clock.
5 Paint the pupil black, and soften it with your brush half on the black and half on the iris color. Pull the brush one time in one direction. If you need to do it again, wipe the brush first.
6 Add a dash of white on top of the iris highlight and at 10 o'clock on the pupil. Outline the eye with Black.

The whites of the eyes are never pure white. Use gray or lavender with a lighter spot in the center. Add lashes after the eye is dry. For more detail in the eye, add flecks of Raw Sienna, blue or green. You can add tiny lines from the edge of the iris to the pupil if you're painting a very large eye.

FUR STROKES

To paint the fur, hold your brush straight up. Use long strokes for the long hair (on the neck and body) and short ones for the short hair (on the muzzle and the top of the head). Follow the direction in which the hair grows in each section, and overlap strokes.

FUR MADE WITH A WISP BRUSH

FUR MADE WITH A COMB BRUSH

1 2 3

NOSE DETAIL

1 Base Paint the Nose
Base paint the nose with medium gray (Black + Titanium White), indicating placement of the nostrils.

2 Outline and Highlight
Outline around the nose and down the center using Black. Fill in the nostrils with Black. Add highlights on the top of the nose and the nostrils with light gray (Black + Titanium White).

3 Soften and Sharpen
Soften the outline by pulling color away from the nose a bit, and sharpen the highlights.

(General painting instructions continued from page 59)
3 Refine the Fur
Apply fur strokes on top of the fur block-in with a comb or wisp brush (see Color Mix Formulas below and Fur Strokes on opposite page). Start by applying the fur strokes on top of the same color, using gradually lighter and lighter values. Pull a few strokes back and forth in the different values. Use fewer strokes with each value change.

COLOR MIX FORMULAS

FUR OVERSTROKES
Light: Naples Yellow
Medium: Burnt Sienna + Raw Sienna
Dark: Burnt Umber + Black

3

German Shorthaired Pointer

PAT WEAVER

MEDIUM: *Watercolor*

COLORS: **Da Vinci:** *Aureolin (Mixture) • Burnt Sienna • Permanent Rose • Ultramarine Blue •* **Shiva Casein:** *Titanium White*

BRUSHES: **Loew-Cornell:** *Series 7020 Golden Taklon Ultra round nos. 10 & 12 (Unless otherwise specified, use large brushes to paint large areas and smaller brushes for small ones.)*

OTHER SUPPLIES: *Cold-pressed watercolor paper, 140 lb. (300gsm)*

artist's comment

Very often, I will do a direct painting with no drawing. This is the case with the black-and-white study of this regal pointer. The painting is just painted on regular sketch paper, but it is very helpful practice as it familiarizes me with the subject.

DOGS

1 Underpaint the Head
Underpaint the head with a soft lavender-gray mix made from Ultramarine Blue + Permanent Rose + a touch of Burnt Sienna. Paint the warm areas with Permanent Rose and Aureolin.

2 Underpaint the Darker Areas and Add the Eyes
Underpaint the darker areas of the face with a mix of Burnt Sienna + Ultramarine Blue. Paint the eyes with a mix of Aureolin + Ultramarine Blue. Add the gray under the neck with a mix of Burnt Sienna + Ultramarine Blue.

3 Develop the Face, Features and Fur
(See the completed painting on the opposite page.) Darken the value of the Burnt Sienna + Ultramarine Blue mix (use less water, more pigment) and further define the darker areas of the face. Paint a thin wash of Burnt Sienna + a bit of Ultramarine Blue over the lavender areas.

Paint the highlight in the eye with White Casein, and add a touch of White Casein + gray (Burnt Sienna + Ultramarine Blue) to the nose. Go back one more time into the neck area with a slightly darker value of the gray mix, leaving some of the original color showing. Add a few little calligraphic marks on the neck to represent fur.

Chocolate Labrador Retriever Puppy

ELAINE BALSLEY

MEDIUM: *Acrylic*

COLORS: **Winsor & Newton Finity Artists' Acrylic Colors:** *Burnt Umber • Dioxazine Purple • Gold Ochre • Mars Orange • Naples Yellow • Payne's Gray • Permanent Alizarin Crimson • Raw Sienna • Titanium White*

BRUSHES: **Loew-Cornell:** *round no. 5/0* • **Princeton:** *acrylic bright no. 8 • round nos. 6 & 10*

OTHER SUPPLIES: *Fredrix Canvas Pad sheet • pencil • Liquitex Acrylic Glazing Medium (for lubricating brush instead of water and to apply after each paint layer is dry) • Liquitex Acrylic Glo... Medium & Varnish (to cover final painting) • water (to clean brushes)*

1 Make a Sketch

I made this graphite sketch from a photo of our then seven-month-old chocolate Labrador retriever puppy named Cocoa. Be particularly careful to place the eyes, nose and snout correctly. Don't worry about the pencil lines showing; they will be covered by the acrylics.

2 Begin Painting Lights and Darks

A chocolate Lab isn't just brown; there are glints of golds and reds in Cocoa's coat. Dip your no. 8 bright into Payne's Gray and Burnt Umber, with a hint of Dioxazine Purple, to begin applying the darker areas and shadows. The purple adds richness to the grays and dark browns, and it helps achieve depth in the shading and shadows. Apply Permanent Alizarin Crimson in some of the darker areas as well. Use shades of Raw Sienna, Gold Ochre and Mars Orange to start the lighter areas. Colors may be mixed on your palette as well as on the canvas as you go. To make the dog appear three-dimensional, remember that darks make areas recede and lights bring areas forward.

artist's comment

Some artists say that acrylics dry too fast for them, but I've found that using an acrylic glaze instead of water to thin the paints allows them to flow better and stay moist longer. And, I like the fact that the paints *do* dry fast so I can keep going with a piece, especially when things are coming together well. Here are a few additional tips:

- It's best to work dark to light, but this is not a hard-and-fast rule.
- Acrylics tend to dry darker. It may be necessary to go back into your painting to touch up the lighter areas. Using glazing medium when applying the paint and in between layers will help with this.
- If you make a mistake, just paint over it. If you make a *really* big mistake, apply gesso (acrylic primer) to regain your surface and start over.

Chocolate Labrador Retriever Puppy

3 Continue Building Form and Begin the Eyes
Continue developing the darks (using Burnt Umber, Payne's Gray, Dioxazine Purple and Permanent Alizarin Crimson) and the lights (using Raw Sienna, Gold Ochre and Mars Orange) to build the form of the puppy. Use the no. 8 bright for larger areas and the nos. 6 and 10 rounds for the smaller areas. For really tight areas and detail, use the no. 5/0 round. Block in the eyes with Naples Yellow.

4 Develop the Coat and Eyes
Use the same colors mentioned in step 3 to continue developing the lights and darks of the coat. I worked more on the right side in this example so you can see the progress. Develop the eyes following the instructions below.

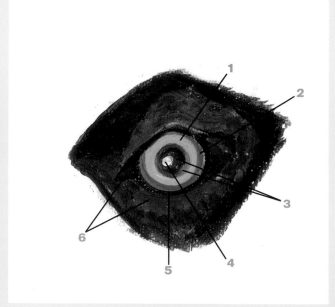

1 Paint the iris Naples Yellow using a no. 6 or 5/0 round.
2 Paint the outer part of the iris with a blend of Gold Ochre + Raw Sienna.
3 Paint the pupil with Burnt Umber. Apply light Payne's Gray around the outside of the pupil.
4 Bring the eye to life by adding a dot of Titanium White for the reflection of light on the pupil.
5 Use Burnt Umber + Payne's Gray to paint the outline of the iris.
6 Mix a little Permanent Alizarin Crimson + Titanium White + a touch of Naples Yellow to add some pink to the corners of the eye and the outer edges beyond the eye.

EYE DETAIL

5 Add Shine to the Coat and Finish the Nose and Details
Concentrate on making the coat shine, adding more details with the 5/0 round. Apply various combinations of Titanium White, Naples Yellow, Gold Ochre and Raw Sienna to break up the lights so they don't all look the same. For a realistic look, aim for a salt-and-pepper effect, letting some of the dark colors in the coat show through instead of merely painting a solid light area across the dark coat. For instance, you might add a few strokes with a little Titanium White + Naples Yellow, or Gold Ochre + a little Raw Sienna.

Paint the snout and nose following the instructions below. When you are finished with the painting, apply a coat of gloss medium and varnish to bring out the colors and protect the finish.

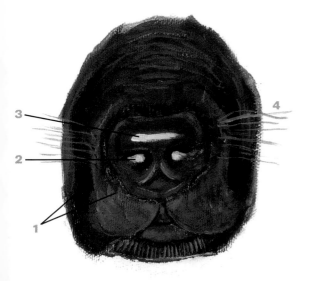

NOSE DETAIL

1 Use darks to make certain areas recede, gradually moving to lighter shades to make the snout and nose appear closer to the viewer.
2 Highlight the nostrils with Titanium White + a little Naples Yellow.
3 Highlight the top of the nose with the same mix to indicate a reflection of light and to bring the nose forward.
4 Add whiskers with Titanium White + Naples Yellow + a touch of Raw Sienna.

artist's comment

If you were painting a dog with a light coat, such as a yellow Lab, you'd want to use darker colors for the whiskers so they can be seen.

Yellow Labrador Retriever Puppies

PAT WEAVER

MEDIUM: *Watercolor*

COLORS: **Da Vinci:** *Aureolin (Mixture) • Burnt Sienna • Permanent Rose • Ultramarine Blue •*
Shiva Casein: *Titanium White*

BRUSHES: **Loew-Cornell:** *Series 7020 Golden Taklon Ultra round nos. 10 & 14 • Series 7700 Golden Taklon*
"Grande" round no. 30 (Unless otherwise specified, use large brushes to paint large areas and
smaller brushes for small ones.)

OTHER SUPPLIES: *Cold-pressed watercolor paper, 140 lb. (300gsm) • old toothbrush • paper towels*

1

2

1 Underpaint the Warm and Cool Areas

There is a lot of white paper left showing in this painting; be sure not to lose the whites as you work. Underpaint the warm areas of the puppies with a mix of Aureolin + Permanent Rose. Underpaint the cool areas with a gray mix of Ultramarine Blue + Permanent Rose + a touch of Aureolin.

2 Paint the Features, Accents, Background and Shadows

Accent the ears with Burnt Sienna, using Burnt Sienna + Ultramarine Blue for the darker areas. Paint the noses and eyes with Ultramarine Blue + Burnt Sienna. Accent the puppies' bodies with slightly darker cool grays and a slightly darker warm mixture.

Alternating between Aureolin, Permanent Rose and Ultramarine Blue, paint the background with a no. 30 round. Paint from the top all the way to the bottom with these three colors, using a lot of water. When the background is dry, paint some shadows behind the dogs' legs with Burnt Sienna and Ultramarine Blue.

3 Develop the Background, Shadows, Accents and Edges

(See the completed painting on the opposite page.) Repaint the background behind the puppies using the same colors (Aureolin, Permanent Rose and Ultramarine Blue), only a little darker. Leave a little of the original underpainting of the background showing between the first shadow shapes (from step 2) and the second darker application of the background.

Continue to repaint the shadow areas, going a little darker and allowing some of the underpainting to show through. Accent the puppies' noses with White Casein. Lose some edges by dipping a toothbrush in water, blotting it on a paper towel and scrubbing lightly to lift a little edge here and there.

Bullmastiff

ERIN O'TOOLE

MEDIUM: *Watercolor*

COLORS: **Holbein:** *Burnt Sienna • Cobalt Blue • Peach Black •* **Winsor & Newton:** *Raw Sienna • Sepia*

BRUSHES: **Isabey:** *kolinsky sable no. 6 •* **Winsor & Newton:** *University Series 233 short handled round no. 1 (Unless otherwise specified, use large brushes to paint large areas and smaller brushes for small ones.)*

OTHER SUPPLIES: *Lanaquarelle cold-pressed paper (use smoother back side) • pencil • Dr. Ph. Martin's Bleed Proof White • Blair Very Low Odor Spray Fixative*

1 Begin the Shadow Areas
After making your pencil drawing, wash Raw Sienna in the shadow areas, then drop in some Cobalt Blue and Burnt Sienna; this will make a purple color. Think about the dog's weight and where the dog touches the ground. Let this dry completely.

2 Add the Body Color and More Shadows
Wet the parts you are going to paint, leaving the highlight areas as dry paper. Lay in a light wash of Raw Sienna on the back, shoulders and head. Deepen the shadows with more Cobalt Blue and Burnt Sienna. Drop in some Sepia on the muzzle. With a fully wet brush, soften the edges where the dog is round. Place the ear shadows and nails with a dark mixture of Sepia, Cobalt Blue and Burnt Sienna.

3 Develop the Head and Finish
(See the Head Detail on this page and the completed painting on the opposite page.) Keep the curve of the eyebrows and creases in the forehead going up. Paint the creases lightly with Sepia warmed with Burnt Sienna. Paint the jowls and beauty marks with Peach Black and Sepia. Keep the plane on the top of the nose light.

Add eye highlights with opaque white. Darken the core shadows (the darkest part of the shadow right next to the highlight). With a thin coat of Sepia, tone down some of the Raw Sienna so it is not so bright.

HEAD DETAIL
The bullmastiff's expression is pensive and expectant, not mean.

Playful Puppy (Australian Shepherd)

ERIN O'TOOLE

MEDIUM: *Watercolor*

COLORS: **Holbein:** *Burnt Sienna* • *Cobalt Blue* • *Peach Black* • **Winsor & Newton:** *Raw Sienna* • *Sepia*

BRUSHES: **Isabey:** *kolinsky sable no. 6* • **Winsor & Newton:** *University Series 233 short handled round no. 1 (Unless otherwise specified, use large brushes to paint large areas and smaller brushes for small ones.)*

OTHER SUPPLIES: *Crescent illustration board* • *sketch paper* • *Dr. Ph. Martin's Bleed Proof White* • *HB pencil* • *ballpoint pen* • *General's charcoal pencil (HB hard)* • *Blair Very Low Odor Spray Fixative*

1 (1)

2 (2)

3 (3)

1 Transfer the Drawing and Paint the First Shapes

Make the drawing on a separate sheet of paper. Rub a soft pencil (HB) on the back of the drawing, then use a ballpoint pen on the front of the drawing to transfer the image to illustration board. Redefine the drawing with charcoal pencil, then spray with fixative before you paint. Begin with a loose wash of warm Peach Black + a little Burnt Sienna to show the round body of the puppy. Use Raw Sienna for the cheeks and eyebrows.

2 Add the Shadows and Black Fur

Paint the shadow areas on the white parts of the puppy with Sepia and a little bit of Cobalt Blue on the muzzle. Add Cobalt Blue to Peach Black for the black fur on the top of the back. Paint the shadow areas with a warm black mix of Peach Black + Burnt Sienna.

3 Develop the Fur

Use large, loose brushstokes of Peach Black over the body for the curly, thick fur. Draw the wispy white hair on the elbow, cheeks and ears with charcoal pencil. Spray with fixative before painting again.

4 Finishing Details and Final Shadow

(See the completed painting on the opposite page.) Use opaque white for the fine whiskers and eye highlights. Use fine brush-strokes of white to define the area between the white ruff and the black back. A slight shadow of Sepia under the feet will ground the puppy on the paper.

artist's comment

Sometimes I scan my sketches and print them to watercolor paper to paint. That way if I mess up a painting, I just print it again and start over. I use an Epson photo ink-jet printer set to handle thicker paper. Use the highest quality scan settings you can when you scan your pencil drawing. Lighten the linework and increase the contrast on the computer. After you've printed onto the watercolor paper, spray lightly with fixative.

Nova Scotia Duck Tolling Retriever

ANNE ARMITAGE

MEDIUM: *Acrylic*

COLORS: **Liquitex Artist Colors:** *Burnt Sienna • Burnt Umber • Cadmium Red Medium • Phthalo Blue (Green Shade) • Raw Sienna • Titanium White • Yellow Oxide*

BRUSHES: **Winsor & Newton:** *Monarch Mongoose Series 5501 bright nos. 0 & 2 • Series 5502 flat nos. 0 & 2 • Series 5503 round no. 00*

OTHER SUPPLIES: *Pencil • disposable palette • Masterson Sta-Wet Handy Palette • spray fixative • Winsor & Newton Artists' Picture Varnish*

1

artist's comment

I mix my paints on a disposable palette and then transfer them to a Masterson Sta-Wet Handy Palette. This is invaluable when working with acrylics, as it will keep your paint wet for days and will help you avoid constant remixing. Also, I prefer synthetic mongoose brushes to sable because they are stiffer and have more spring, making them better suited to the speedy drying time of acrylic.

1 Create the Underpainting

Transfer your drawing to your working surface or draw directly on it. Keep your pencil lines fairly light, and spray the drawing with fixative before you begin painting. In this demonstration, we'll focus on the eye, nose and the fur. Underpaint those areas as follows:

Eyes: Paint with a no. 00 round. Outline the eye using a mix of Burnt Umber + Phthalo Blue. Paint the pupil with Phthalo Blue and a wash of Burnt Umber around the edge. Paint the iris with Yellow Oxide.

Nose: Use your bright brushes to block in the areas of color: Titanium White + a small amount of Cadmium Red Medium for the light areas, and this mixture + a small amount of Phthalo Blue for the dark areas. Use Burnt Umber for the nostrils.

Fur: Block in your colors (see the Color Mix Formulas below), keeping your lines on the left side straight and with little color variation. This is the dog's undercoat being exposed by the blowing wind. Use the bright brushes, as they are fairly stiff and allow you to move color around quickly. Don't forget to paint in the direction of the fur.

When painting a thick coat like this one, I find it really helps to paint the dark shapes first. Be aware of minor variations in fur color. Notice that in this dog some light areas are very yellow (Titanium White + Yellow Oxide), and some areas are pinker (Titanium White + Burnt Sienna).

COLOR MIX FORMULAS

Darkest Fur: Burnt Umber
Dark Fur: Burnt Sienna + Burnt Umber + Raw Sienna (1:1:1)
Medium Fur: Raw Sienna + Burnt Sienna (1:1)
Light Fur: Titanium White + a bit of Medium Fur Mix; Titanium White + a bit of Raw Sienna; Titanium White + a bit of Yellow Oxide; Titanium White + a bit of Burnt Sienna

Nova Scotia Duck Tolling Retriever

2

2 Build Up the Colors and Refine the Fur Shapes

In this step it is important to work from the bottom to the top. You will be building up the fur, and the top hairs should fall over the bottom as they do on a dog's coat. On the thicker parts of the neck, use the flat brushes, as they hold more paint. Use the edge of your bright brushes for the short hairs on the face and legs.

Eyes: Paint with a no. 00 round. Use more Phthalo Blue for the pupil, followed with a wash of Burnt Umber. Build up the color in the iris by applying a very wet wash of Yellow Oxide around the pupil, and a very wet wash of Burnt Sienna around the outside edge.

Nose: Paint with a no. 00 round. Build up the color and add definition. For the darker edge around the outside of the nose and under the nostrils, add Burnt Sienna to the Titanium White + Cadmium Red Medium mix. Darken the inside of the nostrils with a mix of Burnt Umber + Phthalo Blue.

Fur: Build up the colors (see the Color Mix Formulas on page 75) and start blending the lights and darks on the right side.

artist's comment

When clients call me to commission a painting of their dog, they are always surprised and delighted when I request a visit with the pet. I do this for a number of reasons, one being that I'm able to take a lot of my own photos and check colors with swatches I take along with me. But the main reason is to get to know the personality of the dog and see it interact with the owner. It's important to do this at the dog's home so it is comfortable. I can also find out how the owner pictures the dog and try to translate this into the painting. This can be done in very simple ways: with a tilt of the head, a familiar pose, or a favorite toy. Visiting adds time and mileage to the process, but it pays off in spades when I see the look on the client's face at the presentation of the finished painting.

3

3 Complete the Details

Use a no. 0 bright for most of the details and for a bit of drybrushed texture on the face. Use a no. 00 round for fine fur details such as the whiskers and for adding highlights to the thicker clumps of fur. Build up the fur under the chin and on the neck and shoulder area with a flat brush to give it bulk. The contrast between the darks and lights also will give the area dimension. On the top part of the neck, use a very watery mix to give the fur a fluffy look. When finished, spray your painting with varnish.

Eyes: Apply another wash of Phthalo Blue to the pupil and finish with a few very wet washes of Burnt Umber. Run the final wash of Burnt Umber slightly over the edge of the pupil to soften it. Apply two or three more very wet washes of Yellow Oxide around the pupil, with a thin line of a very wet Burnt Sienna wash along the edge of the eye. Do the two washes at the same time so they will bleed into each other very slightly. At the top edge of the eye, paint a very wet wash of Burnt Umber twice for the shadow created by the eyelid. Just under this shadow, add reflected light. This dog is outdoors, so add a tiny bit of Phthalo Blue to Titanium White and create the line of reflected light with a wet wash two or three times. This allows the colors of the eye to show through. For the line under the eye, use Titanium White + a small amount of Cadmium Red Medium.

Nose: When adding the final layer of colors, use a bright brush to blend the transition from one color to another. Add a few little white dots to the top left of the nose to create texture and highlights. Add a Titanium White edge under the nostrils to give a wet effect. Paint the inside of the nostril with more of the Burnt Umber + Phthalo Blue mix, but soften the edge with a wet Burnt Umber wash.

Fur: Keep building up the lighter undercoat with straight lines, and add more paint to the darker fur. (See the Color Mix Formulas on page 75.) On many double-coated dogs, the hair is actually light and darkens only at the outer tip—shown here where the hair is lifted by the wind. On the area of the neck closer to the head, the effect is more haphazard. The undercoat doesn't show completely, but the upper layers appear more feathery in the blowing wind. To create this fluffy look, keep applying layers of very watery washes. For the shadows in the white ruff of the chest, use a mix of Burnt Umber + Phthalo Blue.

Poodle 1

CINDY AGAN

MEDIUM: *Watercolor*

COLORS: **Winsor & Newton:** *Burnt Sienna • French Ultramarine • Mars Black • Naples Yellow • Payne's Gray • Permanent Rose*

BRUSHES: **Robert Simmons:** *Series 785 white sable round nos. 2 & 4*

OTHER SUPPLIES: *Dr. Ph. Martin's Bleed Proof White*

1 Paint the Fur Shadows and Curls

Lightly indicate the subtle shadows in the fur. Paint tight curls around the eyes and mouth and under the neck, belly and legs with a mix of French Ultramarine + Burnt Sienna using a no. 4 round. Carefully preserve the white of the paper for the lightest value.

2 Drybrush Colors and Deepen the Shadows

Relax your hand and drybrush the following colors separately on the fur, allowing each color to dry before applying the next: Naples Yellow, Permanent Rose, Burnt Sienna, French Ultramarine and Payne's Gray. Continue to deepen the shadows with the mix from step 1 to further give shape to the billowy fur. Painting negatively, drybrush Payne's Gray on the outer edge of the body to break up the "cookie cutter" look.

3 Drybrush the Facial Features

With a no. 2 round, drybrush the eyes, nose and mouth with Mars Black. Mix Payne's Gray + Burnt Sienna to make a golden brown, then paint a touch of this around these facial features. Continue to paint the fur with the rainbow of color from step 2.

4 Paint the Highlights and Finishing Details

(See the completed painting on the opposite page.) Thin the opaque white to a creamy consistency and paint several curly highlights in the fur, overlapping into the areas with color, as well as the fine hairs all along the outer edge of the body. For the highlights in shadow, mix opaque white into the Payne's Gray + Burnt Sienna mix. For the finishing details, work a small section at a time and soften the fur as needed with a damp brush and clean water.

artist's comment

Look closely and you will find a surprising rainbow of color in this snow-white fur. The drybrush technique is ideal when creating a fluffy texture. To drybrush, simply thin your paint with water and blot the excess moisture on a towel. This "dry" brush will give you ultimate control for painting fine details.

Poodle 2

JEANNE FILLER SCOTT

MEDIUM: *Acrylic*

COLORS: *Burnt Sienna • Burnt Umber • Payne's Gray • Raw Sienna • Scarlet Red • Titanium White • Ultramarine Blue • Yellow Oxide (Color names may vary from brand to brand)*

BRUSHES: *Round nos. 1, 3, 5 & 7 • shader no. 10 (Brushes may be either sable or synthetic sable)*

OTHER SUPPLIES: *Gessobord • no. 2 pencil • kneaded eraser • Masterson Sta-Wet Palette • wax paper palette • jar of water • palette knife • paper towels*

1 Establish the Form
Lightly draw the poodle in pencil, using a kneaded eraser to make corrections or lighten lines. Use Payne's Gray thinned with water to establish the form and main lines. Use a no. 3 round for the facial details and a no. 7 round for the broader areas.

2 Paint the Dark-Value Colors and Shadowed Areas
Mix the dark value for the nose, mouth and eye outlines with Burnt Umber + Ultramarine Blue. Paint with a no. 1 round.

Mix a bluish shadow color for the coat with Titanium White, Ultramarine Blue, Burnt Umber and a small amount of Raw Sienna. Then, take a portion of this mixture and add more Burnt Umber and Raw Sienna for the warm brown shadows under the belly, around the ears and chest, and under the tail. Paint with a no. 3 round. With the bluish shadow color, paint the shadowed areas of the poodle with a no. 7 round, using dabbing strokes for the curly coat. For the flowing ear hair, use sweeping, slightly curved strokes.

artist's comment

If you accidentally get too much paint on the painting, wipe it with a clean, dry paper towel. If it's already too dry to wipe off, use a dry no. 10 shader with some of the lighter color to tone it down.

Poodle 2

3 Paint the White Areas of the Poodle and the Details

Mix a pink color for the tongue with Titanium White, Scarlet Red and Raw Sienna. Paint with a no. 1 round. To a small amount of the pink, add some Burnt Umber + a little more Scarlet Red. Use a no. 1 round to paint the shadow on the tongue.

On a piece of dry wax paper, mix a warm white with Titanium White + a bit of Yellow Oxide. Paint the lightest parts of the dog's coat with a no. 5 round, using dabbing strokes. Paint fur texture over the shadowed areas of the coat with a fairly dry brush.

Mix the brown eye color with Burnt Umber + Burnt Sienna. Paint with a no. 1 round. Mix a highlight color for the eyes with Titanium White plus a small amount of the bluish shadow color from step 2. Paint small, curved arcs with a no. 1 round. Mix a highlight color for the nose with a small amount of the bluish shadow color and the Burnt Umber + Ultramarine Blue mix from step 2. Paint with a no. 1 round, blending into the adjacent color.

Begin to add some of the warm brown shadow color from step 2 to the coat. Use a no. 3 round to paint small, dabbing strokes to separate the clumps of hair. As you paint these details, use a separate no. 3 round with the bluish shadow color to blend. For the longer hair on the ears, use sweeping strokes. For darker shadows, such as under the chin and belly, take a little of the warm brown shadow color and add some Burnt Umber.

4 Add Finishing Details

Continue adding warm brown shadow details to the coat. Use a no. 3 round with the bluish shadow color to add details to the white parts of the coat, then blend and soften with a separate no. 3 round and the warm white. Define the feet with no. 1 rounds and the warm white and the shadow colors. With the warm white and a no. 3 round, paint small strokes out from the dog's outline to make the coat look more fuzzy and natural against the background.

Shetland Sheepdog

CINDY AGAN

MEDIUM: *Acrylic*

COLORS: **Golden Fluid Acrylics:** *Burnt Umber Light • Carbon Black • Raw Sienna • Raw Umber • Titanium White • Ultramarine Blue • Yellow Ochre*

BRUSHES: **Dynasty:** *Black Gold round nos. 2, 4 & 6 round •* **Winsor & Newton:** *Sceptre Gold Series 303 liner no. 1*

OTHER SUPPLIES: *pencil*

artist's comment

It is not necessary to paint every hair to make fur look convincing and natural. A carefully placed shadow can give the illusion of a tuft of hair and add dimension. When painting a multicolored coat, blend and overlap each stroke where they meet, in irregular lengths.

1 Underpaint the Fur
After making a drawing, begin with a base color, or underpainting, in a middle value to develop the fur's texture. Block in color with a no. 6 round, using transparent washes of Raw Umber so you don't lose the initial drawing.

2 Add Texture to the Fur
Following the growth pattern in the fur, drybrush a mix of Raw Sienna + Burnt Umber Light using a no. 4 round. This lighter value will add warmth as the texture becomes more defined. Glaze Raw Sienna over a few areas to give a warm glow.

Shetland Sheepdog

3 Add Color to the Fur and Highlights
Introduce the cooler colors in the white fur and in the highlights. With a no. 4 round, paint just a hint of color with Ultramarine Blue. Next, dilute Carbon Black and lightly apply color using short brushstrokes around the muzzle, lengthening them as you move further away.

4 Paint Details and Darken Values
Paint the iris and fine hairs around the eyes with Raw Umber using a no. 2 round. Add the rim around the eyes and pupil with Carbon Black. Apply the tiny blue highlights in the eyes with a mix of Ultramarine Blue + Titanium White. Continue to darken the values, blending and overlapping each color gently into the next to add depth and dimension.

5

5 Finish the Details

Add the finishing touches and details using a no. 1 liner. Drybrush a few hairs with Raw Umber, Carbon Black and a mix of Burnt Umber Light + Yellow Ochre + Titanium White. Also add the highlights with a mix of Ultramarine Blue + Titanium White. To soften the fur, glaze Raw Sienna and the Raw Sienna + Burnt Umber mix over the warm colors; glaze Carbon Black lightly over the cool colors.

Shih Tzu

KAREN HUBBARD

MEDIUM: *Acrylic*

COLORS: **Delta Ceramcoat:** *Autumn Brown • Black • Hippo Grey • Magnolia White • Old Parchment • Quaker Grey •* **Flesh Mix:** *Autumn Brown + Quaker Grey (2:1)*

BRUSHES: *Pure red sable round no. 6 • script liner no. 1 • flat no. 4, ½-inch (13mm) & ¾-inch (19mm)*

OTHER SUPPLIES: *Wet palette • black or gray graphite pencil • very fine sandpaper (such as 600 grit)*

artist's comment

- The fur-stroke technique I refer to in the instructions is done with a flattened round sable brush, slightly thinned paint and long overlapping strokes.
- For instructions on how to do the float technique referred to in some of the steps, see the Artist's Comment on page 7.

1 Base Paint the Dog, Eyes and Nose

Base in the dog with Quaker Grey using the ½-inch (13mm) flat. After letting the painted surface dry completely, sand it smooth. After making a drawing in pencil, basecoat the eyes and nose with Black using the ½-inch (13mm) flat.

2 Begin the Fur

Using a no. 6 round, paint fur strokes of Hippo Grey in all the lighter pattern lines. Then paint Black fur strokes, filling in the ears and darkening some of the Hippo Grey areas.

Shih Tzu

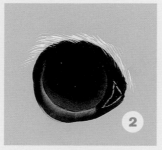

1 Basecoat and Paint the Iris

Basecoat the eye with Black. Paint the iris with a C-stroke of Autumn Brown.

2 Form the Whites

Float Quaker Grey next to the Autumn Brown to form the whites of the eyes.

3 Add Details

Float Hippo Grey across the top of the eye for reflected light. Base in tiny triangles at the corners of the eyes with Flesh Mix.

4 Create Sparkle

Add sparkle dots with Magnolia White.

3 Add Highlights

With a no. 6 round, paint fur strokes of Old Parchment for highlights in the "shine" areas, overlapping brushstrokes lightly into the Hippo Grey and Black areas.

4 "Tuck In" the Lights and Develop the Eyes and Nose

Using the ½-inch (13mm) flat, float Hippo Grey to "tuck in" some areas: under some of the long hairs, above and below the eyes, above the upper edge of the muzzle, around the nose and inside the mouth. Create the iris in the eyes with a C-stroke of Autumn Brown, again using the ½-inch (13mm) flat with side-loaded color. Float Hippo Grey around the edges of the nostrils using the no. 4 flat with side-loaded color.

 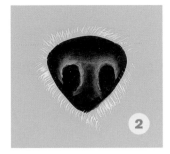 

1 Basecoat and Indicate the Nostrils
Basecoat the nose with Black. Float Hippo Grey around the edges of the nostrils.

2 Brighten the Nostrils
Float Hippo Grey around the nostrils a second time to brighten them.

3 Create Sparkle
Add sparkle dots with Magnolia White.

5 Add Highlights and Feature Details
Using the no. 6 round, paint final highlights with fur strokes of Magnolia White directly over the Old Parchment brushstrokes. Float Quaker Grey with the no. 4 flat, just touching the Autumn Brown, for the whites of the eyes. With the tip of the script liner, paint tiny triangular corners in the eyes with the Flesh Mix. With the no. 4 flat, float Quaker Grey around nostrils a second time to lighten them.

6 Finish With Accents and Sparkle
Paint long accent hairs with the no. 1 script liner, first using Black and then Magnolia White. Have some that curl or cross over, and shorter ones in front of the eyes and around the mouth. Float Hippo Grey with the no. 4 flat across the top of the eye for reflected highlight. Add sparkle dots with Magnolia White and the no. 1 script liner in the eyes and on the nose.

Spaniel 1

LEE HAMMOND

MEDIUM: *Acrylic*

COLORS: *Ivory Black • Titanium White (Color names may vary from brand to brand)*

BRUSHES: *Round nos. 1 & 2 (Brushes may be either sable or synthetic)*

OTHER SUPPLIES: *Graphite pencil • kneaded eraser • ruler • plastic palette • jar of water • canvas paper or panel*

1 Create a Drawing and Paint the Dark Areas

Create an accurate grid-based line drawing (see page 31). When you have removed the grid lines, begin adding details with paint. With a no. 1 round, outline the eyes of the dog with Ivory Black. Fill in the pupil, leaving a small area for the highlight, also called a *catch light*. This catch light is positioned half in the pupil and half in the iris. Switch to a no. 2 round and start filling in the darkest areas of the dog: along the top of the head and on the neck area. Leave the shape of the collar alone.

With a no. 1 round, begin adding strokes to the ears. These brushstrokes should replicate the direction that the fur is growing, and should curve with the waves of the fur. Fill in the nose with the no. 1 round. As for the eyes, leave the highlight areas uncovered.

2 Deepen the Tones and Give Depth to the Face

Continue building the tones of the dog by adding more black with a no. 2 round. The brushstrokes should always follow the direction the fur is going, even if the area fills in solidly. Should brushstrokes show, they must be consistent with the fur's direction. Straight strokes would make the dog's form look flat.

Create a medium gray by mixing Ivory Black + Titanium White. Use this color to fill in the iris of the eyes, the area above and below the eyes, and the area of the muzzle around the nose. Use the same color to fill in the collar. With a few curved strokes using the same gray mix, add some waves to the areas of the ears.

3 Finish the Fur

(See the completed painting on the opposite page.) This step is about creating volume and dimension in the fur. In the previous step, I deliberately left some of the canvas uncovered in the highlight areas. Now you will layer medium gray and Titanium White into these highlight areas to make the fur look dimensional. Using the no. 1 round, add the medium gray in quick, curved strokes to replicate the shape of the waves. To make the waves look shiny, add some white highlights on top of the gray using the same quick strokes. Can you see how this layering technique makes the fur look thick and full?

1

2

Spaniel 2
LIAN QUAN ZHEN

MEDIUM: *Chinese painting ink*

COLORS: **Chinese painting ink or Sumi ink:** *black*

BRUSHES: **Chinese brushes:** *small • large*

OTHER SUPPLIES: *Raw Shuan paper (unsized rice paper), 12" × 15" (31cm × 38cm) • paper towels*

1 Sketch the Dog

Wet the small brush slightly. Sketch the dog using dark ink for the eye and joints of the legs and lighter ink for the rest.

2 Paint the Head

Load the heel of the large brush with light ink, and its middle and tip with dark ink. Hold the brush on its side to paint the ears, then the head and face. Leave the whites created by the sideways brushstrokes as highlights and textures.

3 Paint the Body

Clean the large brush with water, then load it with midtone ink. Hold it straight up to paint the body and the legs in a few strokes. The watermarks between the strokes occur only on this kind of paper, and they are very beautiful effects.

4 Add Darker Ink to the Body

While the midtone ink is wet, use the large brush to pick up a small amount of dark ink to paint the legs and the bottom of the body. The dark ink will blend into the midtone ink, depicting the hair texture.

5 Finish the Body and Details

(See the completed painting on the opposite page.) Immediately use the large brush to paint the hairs on the body. Split its tip by using a paper towel to absorb water from the brush. Then pick up a small amount of dark ink on the split tip to paint the back and belly. Use lighter ink on the rear end and shoulder. Finally, use the small brush to paint the pupil with dark ink.

artist's comment

Splitting the tip of a brush by pressing it between two of your fingers, with a paper towel to absorb excess water, will help you create natural-looking hair texture with every stroke.

Terrier Mix 1

SHERRY C. NELSON

MEDIUM: *Oil*

COLORS: **Winsor & Newton Artists' Oil Colours:** *Burnt Sienna • Cadmium Yellow Pale • Ivory Black • Raw Sienna • Raw Umber • Titanium White • Winsor Red*

BRUSHES: **Sherry C. Nelson:** *Series 303 red sable bright nos. 2, 4 & 6 • Series 312 red sable liner no. 1*

OTHER SUPPLIES: *Pencil • stylus*

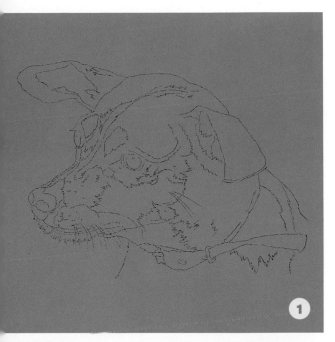

1

1 Transfer the Drawing

Transfer this drawing to your prepared painting surface. Pencil the details completely and carefully, making the drawing as accurate as possible.

2 Base Paint the Features and Fur

Skin area surrounding the eyes: Use a no. 2 bright to base paint Raw Umber mixed with a tiny bit of Titanium White.

Nose: Use a no. 2 or no. 4 bright to base paint with Ivory Black + Raw Umber.

Inner near ear: Using the no. 2 bright, base paint the dark value with Burnt Sienna + Raw Sienna and the light value with Raw Sienna + Titanium White.

Top fold of the near ear: Partially base paint the overlapping fold and the base of the ear with Raw Umber + Raw Sienna, using the no. 2 or no. 4 bright. Add a few strokes of a darker value with Raw Umber + Ivory Black at the bottom tip of the ear.

Far ear: Using the no. 2 bright, base paint the rusty area with Burnt Sienna. Base paint the lightest value with Raw Sienna + Titanium White. Base paint the gray area sparsely with Raw Sienna + Raw Umber.

Mouth: Base paint with Ivory Black + Raw Umber, using the chisel edge of a no. 2 or no. 4 bright to make choppy strokes that indicate the underlying growth direction of the fur.

Muzzle: Base paint sparsely with Ivory Black + Raw Umber, using the no. 4 bright.

Tan eyebrows and the side of the cheek: Using a no. 2 or no. 4 bright, scruff in a sparse, partial coat of Raw Sienna, following the growth direction of the fur in each area.

Ticked fur areas on the face: Using a no. 4 bright, chop in individual strokes of Ivory Black + Raw Umber, following the growth direction of the fur in each area. Leave about 50 percent of the painting surface underneath showing so that when light strokes are added, these underlying darks create areas of fur that vary in value. Using a no. 4 bright, place patches of Raw Umber + Raw Sienna for shading above the collar and below the dark patch on the shoulder.

Collar: Using a no. 4 bright, base paint the dark parts of the collar with Burnt Sienna + Winsor Red. Base paint the light-value areas with Winsor Red. Using a no. 2 bright, base paint the buckle and eyelets with Raw Sienna + Cadmium Yellow Pale.

2

artist's comment

In this demonstration, a plus sign (+) indicates brush-mixed colors. These mixes vary naturally and create a more realistic look. Continue using the same brush type and size in each area unless told to switch to another.

Terrier Mix 1

3 Develop and Blend the Features

Eyes: Fill the eyes in with Ivory Black.

Nose: Draw the lines indicating the nostrils using a stylus.

Inner ear areas: Blend where the light and dark values meet.

Ears: Fill in the remaining dark areas of both ears with Ivory Black + Raw Umber.

Dark head and neck areas: Base paint with Ivory Black + Raw Umber, using a no. 4 or no. 6 bright. Make the edges of these areas broken, with irregular edges echoing the growth direction of the fur in each area.

Collar: To texture the collar, add marks with Burnt Sienna using a no. 2 bright. Shade the buckle areas with Raw Umber.

artist's comment

Fur always has a growth direction. When laying on color, you must pull your brush in the proper direction for the hair to appear realistic. For the body, make many overlapping strokes, beginning from the outer edges of the animal and overlapping hairs as you move inward and upward toward the head. When you begin work on the head, continue to follow the growth direction of the individual areas of hair. You must always work with the lay of the fur for it to appear natural.

4 Add Highlights and Finish Blending

Eyes: Highlight with a dot of white where shown, using the no. 1 liner.

Nose: Highlight the top of the nostrils and a narrow band under each nostril with your dirty brush and Titanium White. Blend the light value to soften into the base coat. Add final highlights with Titanium White.

Inner ear areas: With the chisel edge of your brush, break the edge of the light inner-ear colors into the edges of the dark fur areas, where the values meet.

Ears: Highlight along the edge of each ear where shown with dirty white, using short strokes of the chisel edge of your brush. Blend to connect light and dark values on the ears with the chisel edge, following the growth of the hair.

artist's comment

Different areas of hair or fur will be different lengths, so you must choose the size of your brush and adjust your strokes accordingly. The shortest lengths are often found on the head and face; the longest ones on the chest, belly or tail. Study the length, growth direction, and varied hues and values of a patch of fur before you begin painting it. Choose smaller sizes of brights to more realistically indicate the look of the shorter hair, and use larger brights for the longer hair areas.

Many painters want to take shortcuts when creating hair. One approach is to use a rake or similar brush designed to create a lot of hairs in a single stroke. The problem? This technique often results in too mechanical a look. Hair does not grow with fifteen or twenty hairs lying exactly parallel to each other. For a more realistic look, apply individual strokes using the chisel edge of a bright or round brush.

Terrier Mix 2

SHERRY C. NELSON

MEDIUM: *Oil*

COLORS: **Winsor & Newton Artists' Oil Colours:** *Burnt Sienna • Ivory Black • Raw Sienna • Raw Umber • Titanium White*

BRUSHES: **Sherry C. Nelson:** *Series 303 red sable bright nos. 2, 4 & 6 • Series 312 red sable liner no. 1*

OTHER SUPPLIES: *Pencil • stylus • odorless thinner*

1 Transfer the Drawing

Transfer this drawing to your prepared painting surface. Pencil the details completely and carefully, making the drawing as accurate as possible.

2 Base Paint the Features and Fur

Area surrounding the eyes: Use a no. 2 bright to base paint with Ivory Black + Raw Umber.

Nose: Use a no. 2 or no. 4 bright to base paint the area around the nose and the nostrils with Ivory Black + Raw Umber. Draw the lines indicating the nostrils using a stylus.

Inner ear areas: Base paint with Burnt Sienna and a no. 4 bright.

Top fold of the ears: Partially base paint the overlapping fold of each ear in a dry, scruffy manner using Raw Umber on a no. 2 bright.

Mouth area, eyebrows and the bridge of the nose: Use a no. 2 or no. 4 bright to base paint these areas with Ivory Black + Raw Umber, using the chisel edge to make choppy strokes that indicate the underlying growth direction of the fur in each area. The mouth and eyebrow areas should be more solid, with less of the painting surface showing, while the bridge of the nose should be only partially filled in.

Tan facial areas: Using a no. 4 or no. 6 bright, scruff in a very sparse coat of Raw Sienna, following the growth of the fur in each area.

Dark facial areas: Using a no. 4 or no. 6 bright, sparingly scruff in a dry mix of Ivory Black + Raw Umber, chopping paint in the growth direction of the fur in each area.

artist's comment

In this demonstration, a plus sign (+) indicates brush-mixed colors. These mixes vary naturally and create a more realistic look. Continue using the same brush type and size in each area unless told to switch to another.

Terrier Mix 2

③

3 Develop and Blend the Features

Eyes: Fill the eyes in with Ivory Black. Highlight around the inner edge of the area surrounding the eyes with a mix of Raw Sienna + a bit of dirty Titanium White.

Nose: Highlight the top of the nostrils and a narrow band under each nostril with your dirty brush and Titanium White.

Inner ear areas: Shade where shown inside the ears with Raw Umber. Use a no. 2 bright to highlight along the edges of the ears and the inside ear with Titanium White.

Top fold of the ears: Finish filling in the remainder of the folds with Titanium White, following the growth direction of the fur.

Application of first light-value fur strokes: Load your bright brushes with Titanium White from a sparse loading zone, changing sizes where appropriate for the fur length in each area of the face and head. Begin applying the overlapping strokes on top of the dry base coats you placed in step 2. Don't attempt to fully cover the base coat at this point; just begin creating the proper fur length and growth direction in each area. Where base-coat values meet, apply fur strokes on top of the junction of colors. Where facial fur meets the eye areas, the nose pad and mouth area, and the base of the ears, edge the chisel edge of the brush into those areas to create a connection between the color areas.

(c)2005
~ Sherry C. Nelson ~

4

4 Add Highlights, Blend and Finish the Fur

Eyes: Highlight with a dot of Titanium White where indicated, using the no. 1 liner.

Nose: Blend the light value at the top of the nose to soften it into the base coat. Add the final highlight with Titanium White using the no. 1 liner.

Inner ear areas: Blend the shading color to soften. With the chisel edge of a bright brush, break the edge where the white meets the Burnt Sienna. Highlight along the edge of the ear with Titanium White and short strokes of the chisel edge.

Top fold of the ears: Blend between the light and dark values with the chisel edge of a bright brush, following the direction of the hair growth. With a tapping motion of a brush loaded with a little Titanium White, indicate the very short, stiff hairs that grow along the edges of the ear.

Application of the final fur strokes: Continue adding white fur strokes, gradually building the most dominant areas of the face with more solid applications of paint. Follow the growth direction carefully, and gradually build highlight areas with additional light strokes laid on top of basecoat value. Create final connections between the eyes, mouth, nose and ears by pulling additional light strokes into the edges of those areas. Pull a few hair strokes over the base of the ears, into the edges of the dark eye areas, and even a few from the inner corners of the eyes to extend in front of the eye itself.

Whiskers: Thin a small puddle of Ivory Black + Raw Umber with odorless thinner. With the no. 1 liner, add the few dark whiskers, pulling from the whisker pads outward. Blend the starting point of each whisker with a dry, dirty chisel edge.

Weimaraner Puppy

Jeanne Filler Scott

Medium: *Oil*

Colors: *Burnt Umber • Cadmium Orange • Cadmium Red Medium • Cadmium Yellow Light • Payne's Gray • Permanent Green Light • Raw Sienna • Titanium White • Ultramarine Blue (Color names may vary from brand to brand)*

Brushes: *Round nos. 3 & 8 • filbert no. 2 • flat no. 5 (Brushes may be either sable or synthetic sable)*

Other Supplies: *Gessobord • no. 2 pencil • kneaded eraser • Winsor & Newton Liquin medium • turpentine • palette knife • paper towels*

1 Establish the Form

Lightly sketch the puppy onto the panel with a pencil, using a kneaded eraser to make any corrections. Use Payne's Gray thinned with turpentine and a no. 8 round to paint the main lines and contours.

2 Paint the Dark Values

Mix a warm dark gray with Titanium White + Burnt Umber + Ultramarine Blue. Paint the shadowed parts of the coat with a no. 8 round, using a small amount of Liquin so the paint flows easily. For the broad areas, use a no. 2 filbert.

Mix a warm black for the nose and the pupils of the eyes with Burnt Umber + Ultramarine Blue + a small amount of the warm dark gray mix. Paint them with a no. 8 round.

Mix the green shadow color for the collar with Permanent Green Light + Cadmium Orange + Burnt Umber + a small amount of Titanium White. Paint it with a no. 8 round.

artist's comment

In this demonstration, you will learn how to paint a solid-colored puppy with very short and smooth hair, blending where different values meet to achieve a lifelike look. This is different from painting a multi-colored or longhaired dog, since you will concentrate more on the animal's contour and form.

Weimaraner Puppy

3 Paint the Middle Values
Mix a middle-value gray with Titanium White + Raw Sienna + Ultramarine Blue. Paint the broad areas with a no. 2 filbert and the smaller areas with a no. 8 round. Use just enough Liquin so the paint flows easily. Decrease the pressure on your brush in areas where the values need to be lighter. Blend where the middle-value gray meets the warm dark gray, using a separate brush for each color.

4 Paint the Background and Add Highlights
Mix a bluish gray for the background with Titanium White + Ultramarine Blue + Burnt Umber. Paint thinly, using a no. 5 flat and Liquin with semicircular, dabbing strokes. Switch to a no. 2 filbert for painting around the puppy's contours.

Mix a highlight color for the puppy's coat with Titanium White + a small amount of Raw Sienna. Paint mainly with a no. 2 filbert, using a no. 8 round for smaller detail.

Mix a pinkish color for around the eyes, muzzle, toes, underbelly and side with Titanium White + Cadmium Red Medium + small amounts of Raw Sienna and Cadmium Orange. Mix a lighter green highlight for the collar using a portion of the green shadow color from step 2 + Titanium White + a small amount of Cadmium Yellow Light. Paint all of these areas with a no. 8 round.

5

6

5 Blend the Edges and Add Detail
With separate brushes for each color (no. 2 filberts for broad areas and no. 8 rounds for details), blend the warm, dark-gray shadow color with the middle-value gray. Blend the highlight color with the middle-value color, and the pinkish color with the adjacent color.

6 Continue Blending and Add Finishing Details
Use no. 3 rounds to finish. Continue to blend where one color meets the other.

Mix the blue color for the eyes with Titanium White + Ultramarine Blue + a touch of Cadmium Orange. For the shadowed eye, add a bit of the warm black from step 2. Blend where the pupil and the dark outline around the eye meet the eye color.

Paint the toenails using the pinkish color from step 4 mixed with some of the warm black. Blend the edges with the pinkish color. Use a bit of the blue eye color mixed with a bit of Titanium White to paint the subtle highlight in the right eye as a small arc.

Add whisker detail to the muzzle with a small amount of the warm dark gray from step 2 and blend with the adjacent color.

Details

Getting the overall shape and form correct is important when painting any subject in a realistic way, but the details in an animal painting can instantly distinguish amateurish work from a skillful piece of art. Master the details by following these useful tips for portraying accurate paws, noses, eyes and hair.

Cat Paws

CLAUDIA NICE

MEDIUM: *Watercolor*

COLORS: *Burnt Sienna • Burnt Umber • Cobalt Blue • Dioxazine Purple • Yellow Ochre (Color names may vary from brand to brand)*

BRUSHES: *Round nos. 00 & 4*

OTHER SUPPLIES: *Pencil*

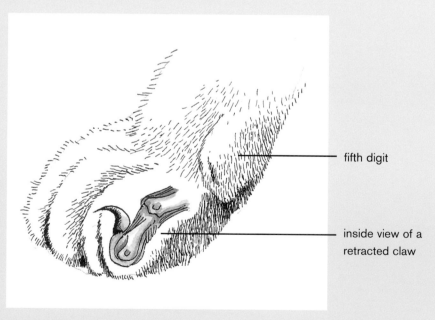

fifth digit

inside view of a retracted claw

RIGHT FRONT FOOT

1 Make a Preliminary
Sketch
Pencil the general shape of
the foot, including the fifth
digit (see the Artist's Comment).

2 Draw the Toes
Draw the individual toes
and the claw sheaths. Notice
that in this side view, the
fourth toe is mostly hidden.

3 Apply an Overall Wash
Mix Yellow Ochre + Burnt
Sienna. Mute the resulting
burnt orange by adding a
touch of Cobalt Blue, then
thin the mix with water to
create a pale wash. Using a
no. 4 round, apply this wash
over the foot, except for the
toe tips which should be left
white. Let dry.

4 Add Shadows
and Blend
Apply a second layer of
the mix from step 3 to the
shadow areas. For a browner
tone, add more Cobalt Blue.
Blend and soften the edges
with a clean, damp brush.
Let dry.

artist's comment

Cat paws usually have four toes; however, some cats have more. Front paws
have an extra digit above the paw on
the inside of the leg. Hair direction is
downward, running from the body to
the toes.

5 Paint Detail Hairs
Use a no. 00 round to
stroke individual hairs over
the paw. Use the mix from
step 3 as a starting point,
darkening or lightening the
color as needed, depending
on whether you are painting
hairs in shadow or in light.

DETAILS

Cat Paws

DETAILS

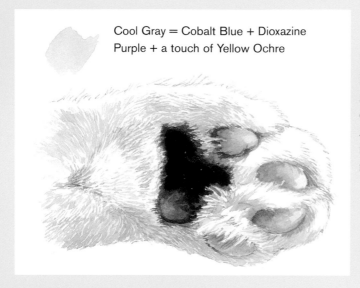

Cool Gray = Cobalt Blue + Dioxazine Purple + a touch of Yellow Ochre

UNDERSIDE OF A HIND PAW

NOTICE HOW THE HAIR CHANGES DIRECTION AROUND THE PADS AND REVERSES ITSELF ON THE BOTTOM OF THE FOOT.

TABBY STRIPES ON A LEFT HIND LEG

GINGER (ORANGE) TABBY STRIPES ON A HIND LEG IN A SITTING POSITION

Burnt Sienna + Yellow Ochre

with a touch of Cobalt Blue added

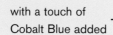

chocolate point coloration (Add a touch of Cobalt Blue to Burnt Umber.)

WHITE FOREPAWS IN A RELAXED POSITION

LEFT FRONT PAW

Dog Paws

CLAUDIA NICE

MEDIUM: *Watercolor*

COLORS: *Burnt Umber • Cobalt Blue • Dioxazine Purple • Neutral Tint • Sap Green • Sepia • Yellow Ochre (Color names may vary from brand to brand)*

BRUSHES: *Round nos. 00 & 4*

OTHER SUPPLIES: *Pencil*

Distant feet show little detail.

WHITE GERMAN SHEPHERD

Dog Paws

Dew claw

PAINTING HAIR

1 Apply the Base Wash
Apply a wash of Yellow Ochre.

2 Add Shading
Shade with a mix of Yellow Ochre + Dioxazine Purple.

3 Add Hairs
Stroke in the hairs with light and dark variations of the mix from step 2 using a no. 00 round.

PAINTING PADS

1 Apply the Base Wash
Begin with a wash of Sepia. Let dry.

2 Add Shading
Shade with a second wash of Sepia.

3 Create Texture
Texture the pad by tapping diluted Sepia over it with the tip of a no. 00 round.

artist's comment

Dog paws have four toes, with an extra digit called a dew claw located on the inside of the front leg, just above the foot.

PAINTING A DETAILED PAW

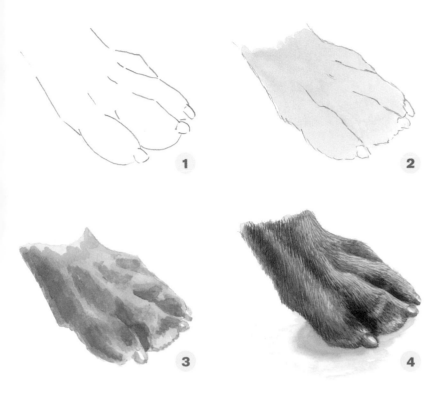

1 Make a Drawing
Lightly draw the paw in pencil. This is a right front foot.

2 Paint an Overall Wash
Mix a wash of Burnt Umber toned down with a touch of Dioxazine Purple. Apply the wash evenly with a no. 4 round. Leave highlight areas on the claws.

3 Add Shading
Shade the paw with a second layer of the mix from step 2 in the shadow areas. Add a little Sap Green to the mix for the deepest tones.

4 Add Hairs and a Cast Shadow
Use a no. 00 round to stroke individual hairs over the foot. Follow the hair growth direction, which is downward from the leg toward the tips of the toes. Use Neutral Tint to add a cast shadow to help tie the foot to the ground and further establish the light direction.

White paws are left unpainted except in the shadow areas.

The off-white shadows are Cobalt Blue + Dioxazine Purple muted with Yellow Ochre.

Short Fur on a Tortoiseshell Cat

CINDY AGAN

MEDIUM: *Acrylic*

COLORS: **Golden Fluid Acrylics:** *Burnt Umber Light* • *Carbon Black* • *Raw Sienna* • *Raw Umber* • *Titan Buff*

BRUSHES: **Dynasty:** *Black Gold round no. 6* • **Winsor & Newton:** *Sceptre Gold Series 303 liner no. 2*

OTHER SUPPLIES: *Paper towels*

1

artist's comment

The key to painting the texture in short fur is to closely observe the direction the fur is growing and the bone structure beneath the fur. Establish a basic pattern and simply continue to build on that.

1 Lightly Paint the Fur Pattern

Load a no. 6 round with thinned Raw Umber and gently flatten the brush on a paper towel. Turn the brush on its side and begin painting the fur in quick, short strokes. Take care to follow the growth pattern in the fur.

2 Go Over the Fur With a Darker Color

With more confidence now in the placement of this fur, repeat step 1 using slightly diluted Carbon Black. Paint the hairs in a somewhat irregular manner to make the fur look more convincing. Lift the brush off the paper completely with each stroke to avoid drag marks.

3 Add an Overall Wash and Fine Hairs

Mix Burnt Umber Light + Raw Sienna for a golden brown. Paint a thin wash of this mix over the fur and let it dry completely. Then use a no. 2 liner to add fine hairs with a more concentrated application of color. Paint these fine hairs from left to right, slightly overlapping each stroke for a natural look.

4 Blend the Color

Use Raw Umber and a no. 2 liner to blend the color in the fur. With very little water in the brush, begin in the center of the dark fur and pull the brush down toward the light-colored fur. Vary the length of the brushstrokes.

5 Add Shadows and Highlights

(See the completed step on the opposite page.) Deepen the shadow on the right side and throughout the painting as needed with Carbon Black. Add Titan Buff to the golden brown mix from step 3, then paint a few highlights on the very tips of the hairs that are catching the light.

2

3

4

Long Hair on a Cocker Spaniel

CINDY AGAN

MEDIUM: *Watercolor*

COLORS: **Winsor & Newton:** *Burnt Umber • Sepia • Van Dyke Brown*

BRUSHES: **Robert Simmons:** *Series 785 white sable round nos. 2, 4 & 6*

OTHER SUPPLIES: *Dr. Ph. Martin's Bleed Proof White • pencil • kneaded eraser • facial tissue*

1 Begin the Darkest Values

After making a drawing, squint your eyes to find the shadows in the hair and loosely block in these dark values with Van Dyke Brown and a no. 6 round. Soften the edges of the brushstrokes with a clean, damp brush using a graded wash (see the Artist's Comment).

2 Repeat With Darker Color

Lighten the pencil lines with a kneaded eraser before adding more color. Too much pigment can "lock in" the pencil and make it difficult to lift. Repeat step 1, but apply the color a little darker this time.

3 Create Form and Definition

Define the shape and form of the body part you are painting with a no. 4 round and Van Dyke Brown, painting the strands of hair in more detail. Once this is dry, deepen the shadows with a touch of Sepia to create depth. Save the white of the paper for the lightest values. Glaze Burnt Umber at the edges of these highlights to add warmth.

4 Refine the Hair

Check the range of values and deepen them with the colors from step 3 as needed. Glaze Burnt Umber lightly and directly over the top of any dark hair that needs softening. Use clean water to soften any hard edges adjacent to the lightest hair.

5 Add Light Strands and Wispy Hairs

(See the completed section of the finished painting on the opposite page.) Thin the opaque white with just a touch of water and, with a no. 2 round, add a few light strands of hair overlapping into the medium values. Mix opaque white with Burnt Umber for the wispy hairs over the darkest values. If the opaque white paint, alone or in a mix, appears too bright or unnatural, simply soften it with a damp brush and blot with a tissue.

artist's comment

A key ingredient to painting long hair realistically is to soften any hard edges using a graded wash. This avoids that stiff "straw" look. To paint a graded wash, apply a thin glaze (layer) of color, rinse the brush, blot the excess water with a tissue and start pulling the color until it fades out.

Curly Hair on a Springer Spaniel

Erin O'Toole

Medium: *Oil*

Colors: **Gamblin:** *Flake White Replacement • Ivory Black • Phthalo Blue •* **Winsor & Newton:** *Burnt Umber • Cadmium Red • Cadmium Yellow*

Brushes: **Silver Brush:** *Grand Prix bristle round nos. 2 • bristle filbert nos. 2 & 4 •* **Winsor & Newton:** *sable round no. 2 •* **Other:** *large flat brush, such as a 2-inch (51mm) housepainting brush*

Other Supplies: *Strathmore bristol board (3-ply, vellum finish) • white acrylic gesso • Gamblin Neo Meglip painting medium • General's charcoal pencil (HB hard) • Blair Very Low Odor Spray Fixative • Saral transfer paper or light table • wooden support • tape*

artist's comment

The best part about English springer spaniels is their ears. The fur on them is long, curly and black. I used two versions of black, a warm one and a cool one, to give them form.

1 Begin With Cool Shadows

Coat your bristol board with white acrylic gesso, then transfer your sketch to the board using a light table or transfer paper. Define the drawing with charcoal pencil, then spray with fixative. Using the no. 4 filbert, paint the darks in the shadow side of the dark fur with Ivory Black + a small amount of Phthalo Blue thinned with painting medium. Use the no. 2 filbert and Flake White + Phthalo Blue + a touch of Burnt Umber for the shadow side of the white fur. Use Cadmium Yellow + Burnt Umber for the top part of the eye; mix in some Cadmium Red for the bottom part of the eye.

2 Add Warm Lights

Use the no. 2 filbert with Flake White and a touch of Cadmium Yellow for the light side of the white fur. With the no. 2 bristle round, apply warm black (Ivory Black + Cadmium Red) for the lighter areas of black fur. Paint the nails using warm black and the no. 2 sable round. Add shadow lines under the legs with cool black (Ivory Black + thinned Phthalo Blue).

3 Define the Ears and Muzzle

Define where the ears start on the head with a cool gray (Phthalo Blue + Ivory Black + Flake White). Soften the muzzle and begin to define the mouth with the no. 2 bristle round. Use Cadmium Yellow with Burnt Umber to separate the legs from the background. Using a no. 2 sable round, paint the eye highlight with Cadmium Yellow and a small amount of Burnt Umber.

4 Develop the Curls and Details

(See the completed step on the opposite page.) Use the no. 2 bristle round to paint the curls on the ears. Make some of them warm (Cadmium Red + Ivory Black) and others cool gray using the mix from step 3. Using the no. 2 sable round, paint a few curls of fur on the chest and cheek with cool gray. Add some freckles to the nose with warm black. Keep the muzzle soft-looking by dragging some gray across the outline with the no. 4 filbert.

Cat & Dog Noses

CATHY JOHNSON

MEDIUM: *Acrylic*

COLORS: *Payne's Gray • Quinacridone Red • Titanium White (Color names may vary from brand to brand)*

BRUSHES: *Flat ½-inch (12mm) • sharp round no. 3*

OTHER SUPPLIES: *HB pencil*

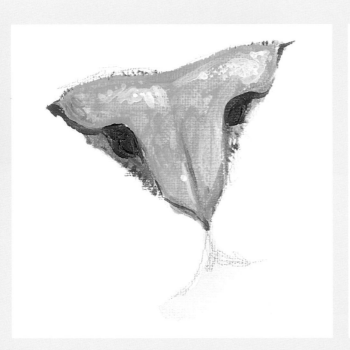
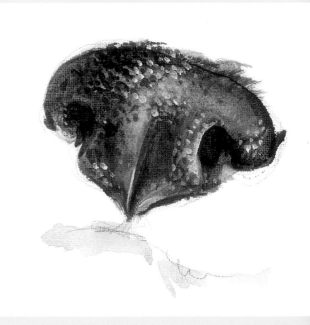

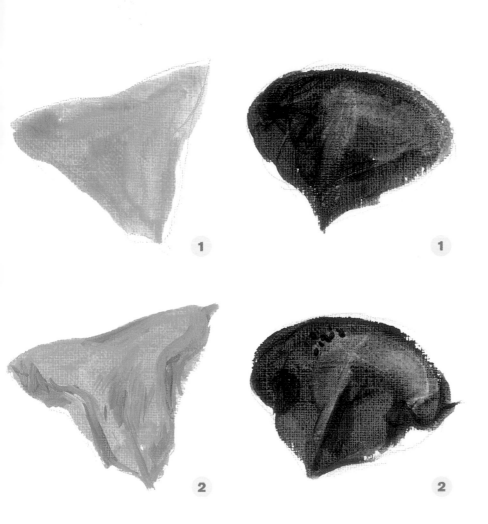

1 Sketch and Paint the First Layer

Sketch the basic shape of the nose with an HB pencil. Cats generally have a more triangular nose, while a dog's is somewhat more rounded. With a flat brush, lay in the first layer of color with bold, quick, sure strokes, following the shape of the nose. For the cat nose, mix Quinacridone Red with Titanium White for a soft pink; for the dog nose, cut the Payne's Gray with a very small amount of Titanium White to lighten the value a bit in the highlight areas. Also, lift a bit of pigment to highlight its rounded shape before the paint dries.

2 Develop the Form

With a flat brush, start building up the dark shapes and defining details such as the nostrils and creases, using thin-ner glazes of paint if you wish. Add a bit of Payne's Gray to the existing pink mixture to form these details on the cat; for the dog, use a stronger, more opaque mix of Payne's Gray to suggest the texture and details.

3 Finish With Details

(See the completed steps for each nose on the opposite page.) With the round brush and Payne's Gray straight from the tube, paint the final dark, sharp details. Add a bit of pure Titanium White where the moist noses catch the light. On the dog nose, the texture is more noticeable, so apply color with a light touch using the tip of the brush in a quick dot-ting motion. For the cat nose, apply tiny strokes with the tip of the brush.

artist's comment

Of course, all dogs don't have black noses, nor do all cats have pink ones, so adjust the colors to suit your subject.

Eyes on a Tabby Cat

CINDY AGAN

MEDIUM: *Acrylic*

COLORS: **Golden Fluid Acrylics:** *Burnt Umber Light • Carbon Black • Fluid Sap Green Hue • Payne's Gray Raw Sienna • Raw Umber • Titanium White*

BRUSHES: **Winsor & Newton:** *Sceptre Gold Series 303 liner no. 1 •* **Robert Simmons:** *Series 785 round no. 2*

OTHER SUPPLIES: *pencil*

1 Preserve the Drawing and Frame the Eye
After making a detailed drawing, thin Carbon Black to a medium gray and outline the iris to preserve the drawing using a no. 1 liner. Paint the tiny hairs around the eyes with Raw Umber and an earth-tone mix of Raw Sienna + Burnt Umber Light.

2 Begin the Iris and Paint the Pupil
Using a no. 2 round, cover the entire iris with a very light glaze of Sap Green and allow to dry. Use the earth-tone mix from step 1 to indicate the golden brown highlights in the iris. Paint the vertical pupils with Carbon Black.

3 Develop Shadows and Light Areas
Add some deep values in the shadows around the pupil with a no. 2 round and Sap Green, as well as a mix of Sap Green + Carbon Black. For the lighter value, mix Sap Green + Titanium White + a touch of Raw Sienna.

4 Define and Blend
Define the iris by carefully outlining it using a no. 1 liner and Carbon Black. Blend a few tiny hairs outside this edge and into the fur. To soften the color inside the black outline in the iris, wet a small section at a time and gently blend either the greens or the earth tones.

5 Add Highlights and Flecks of Color
(See the completed section of the finished painting on the opposite page.) Now create that important "sparkle" in the eyes using a no. 2 round and Titanium White. Place the white where the brightest light reflects in the iris, and blend softly. Mix a touch of Titanium White + Payne's Gray for the more subtle highlights. Finish with a few "flecks" or dots of color around the pupil with the green mixtures from step 3 and the earth tones from step 1.

artist's comment

When painting cats, my personal favorite feature—and undoubtedly the most important—is the eyes. I often save them (the best!) for last and look forward to the challenge. Each set of cat eyes is wonderfully unique in color, markings and expression.

About the Artists

CINDY AGAN

Cindy Agan is a self-taught and internationally published watercolor and portrait artist. She prefers realism in all mediums she uses, which include pastel, watercolor and, most recently, fluid acrylics. She is the author of a book and video titled *Painting Watercolors That Sparkle With Life* (North Light Books). Her award-winning paintings have been featured in several publications and books, including North Light's best-of-watercolor *Splash* series, volumes 6, 7 and 9. Cindy's work has been displayed in numerous national and international juried shows and can be found in private and corporate collections. She teaches workshops throughout the country. Visit www.cindyaganart.com.

ANNE ARMITAGE

Anne Armitage works full-time doing commission work of pets—mainly dogs, cats and horses—for her company, Picture Perfect Pets. She also sells prints of birds, wolves and horses in stores and galleries around Ottawa Valley, Ontario.

ELAINE BALSLEY

Elaine Balsley inherited her mother's love of art and enjoys painting everything from landscapes to portraits in many different mediums, including acrylic, watercolor and pastel. Without a formal art education, she fortified her knowledge with various art classes over the years and has studied under Ron Lee, a professional illustrator and fine artist at the Wind Art Gallery in Centerville, Ohio. She is particularly inspired by the Impressionists.
Visit www.orchardviewstudio.com/mypage.html.

SHARRON ENGLAND

Sharron England has been teaching painting since 1980. She has taught at national, Heart of Ohio Tole (HOOT) and Las Vegas conventions for many years, and has conducted classes in Japan and Italy as well. She received certification from the National Society of Decorative Painters in 1992, and in 1993 she published a book titled *Animal Lifelike Painting*.

BONNIE FREDERICO

Bonnie Frederico has always loved art, but started her professional career as a math teacher. Her ability to teach led her into the decorative art field. In 1994, she became a Certified Decorative Artist. Bonnie teaches at home and at conventions in the U.S. and Canada. Her work has been published in several painting magazines and she is the author of North Light Books title *Fresh and Easy Watercolors for Beginners*.
Visit www.sellarshop.com.

LEE HAMMOND

Polly "Lee" Hammond is an illustrator and art instructor from the Kansas City area. She owns and operates a private art studio called Take It to Art, where she teaches realistic drawing and painting. Lee has been an author with North Light Books since 1994. Among her many North Light titles are *Acrylic Painting With Lee Hammond*, *Drawing Realistic Pets From Photographs* and *Drawing in Color: Animals*. She also writes and illustrates articles for such publications as *The Artist's Magazine*, and she illustrates children's books. Contact Lee at pollylee@aol.com or visit www.leehammond.com.

PEGGY HARRIS

Peggy Harris of Nashville, Tennessee, is the author of numerous bestselling books and five videos on painting baby animals, featuring her trademark technique for creating fur and feathers. Her newest book is *Painting Nature*, published by North Light Books. Visit www.peggyharris.com.

KAREN HUBBARD

Karen Hubbard has always loved birds and other animals. She started painting in oils and then began working in acrylics and watercolor as well. Karen earned her Certified Decorative Artist distinction in 1988 and has won numerous awards in art shows with her animal paintings. She has authored four wildlife painting books and more than 150 pattern packet designs of birds, wildlife and pets. Based in Oregon, she has taught many workshops over the past thirty years in the U.S., Canada, England, Taiwan and Japan.

CATHY JOHNSON

Cathy Johnson has worked with the editors and art directors of a number of publishers, creating illustrations in a variety of mediums. She has written thirty books on art, history and natural history subjects, a number of magazine articles, as well as regular columns for *Country Living*, *The Artist's Magazine* and *Watercolor Magic* (where she is a contributing editor). She is the author of seven North Light books for artists, including *Drawing and Painting Animals*, *Creating Textures in Watercolor*, and the bestselling *Watercolor Tricks and Techniques*. She also authored the *Sierra Club Guide to Sketching in Nature* and the *Sierra Club Guide to Painting in Nature*.
Visit www.cathyjohnson.info and
www.cafepress.com/cathy_johnson.

GAYLE LAIBLE

Gayle Laible is a Certified Decorative Artist and was art director for WLW-TV/Radio, serving Cincinnati, Dayton and Columbus, Ohio, for thirteen years. For twenty-four years she owned The Nearsighted Owl, an art store, studio, framing shop and gallery. Gayle and her cousin, Sharon Saylor, own Sharon & Gayle Publications, Inc., publishers of how-to-paint books.

SHERRY C. NELSON

Sherry C. Nelson is a Master of Decorative Arts who teaches in seminars and conventions worldwide. Known throughout the field of decorative painting for her realistic portrayals of birds and other wildlife, she has painted and taught wildlife art for more than thirty-five years. An active member of the Society of Decorative Painters since its founding in 1972, she is a past president of the organization and received the prestigious Silver Palette Award in recognition of her promotion of decorative painting worldwide. Sherry has produced over twenty publications to date. Visit www.sherrycnelson.com.

CLAUDIA NICE

Claudia Nice attended the University of Kansas but gained her realistic pen, ink and watercolor techniques from sketching nature. A native of the Pacific Northwest, she spent more than fifteen years traveling across North America as an art consultant, conducting seminars, workshops and demonstrations. Claudia is the author of several North Light books, including *Creating Textures in Pen & Ink With Watercolor* and *Watercolor Made Simple With Claudia Nice*.

ERIN O'TOOLE

Erin O'Toole has filled journals with images of birds and flowers for over twenty-five years and is the author of North Light Books' *Create Your Own Artist's Journal*. Erin's watercolors, including over 500 botanicals for the Western and National Garden books, appear in many Sunset and Audubon books.

JEANNE FILLER SCOTT

Jeanne Filler Scott is nationally recognized for her paintings of animals, both domestic and wild. She is the author and illustrator of the North Light books *Painting Animal Friends* and *Wildlife Painting Basics: Small Animals*. She is a member of the prestigious Society of Animal Artists, an international organization based in New York City, and a signature member of the Worldwide Nature Artists Group, an international society of world-class nature artists dedicated to celebrating and preserving the natural world. Visit www.jfsstudio.com.

MAUREEN SHIER

Maureen Shier affectionately refers to pets as "fur babies." Her passion for animals is evident in the great detail she adds to most of her work. She is known for her ability to teach others simple techniques for painting their pets. Maureen has had several designs published internationally in magazines, books, CD books, patterns and a DVD/video series on animal painting techniques. Visit www.moeshier.com.

PENNY SOTO

Penny Soto has won over 250 awards and has exhibited widely, including at the San Francisco World Trade Center, the Triton Museum of Art and the Pacific Bell Corporation. Twenty-six of her mural-size paintings appear in the permanent art collection display in Nordstrom stores throughout the U.S. She writes for many art magazines and authored *Paint Glowing Colors in Watercolor*, published by North Light Books.

PAT WEAVER

Pat Weaver is an international watercolor instructor who has received numerous awards for her work from watercolor societies, universities, businesses and more. She also has extensive publication credits including features in *American Artist*, *Watercolor Magic* and the best-of-watercolor book *Splash 7*. She is the author of North Light Books title *Watercolor Simplified*.

LIAN QUAN ZHEN

Lian Quan Zhen teaches Chinese and watercolor painting workshops internationally. His paintings hang in numerous institutional and private collections, including the MIT Museum, which has collected fourteen of his paintings. He has published two titles with North Light Books: *Chinese Painting Techniques for Exquisite Watercolors* and *Chinese Watercolor Techniques: Painting Animals*.

Resources

Ampersand Art Supply
Austin, TX; (800) 822-1939
www.ampersandart.com

Blair
www.blairsprays.com

Cheap Joe's Art Stuff
Boone, NC; (800) 227-2788
www.cheapjoes.com

Chinese painting supplies
(See Zhen Studio)

ColArt Americas, Inc.
Piscataway, NJ
(888) 422-7954
www.liquitex.com

Crescent Cardboard
Company, L.L.C.
Wheeling, IL; (800) 323-1055
www.crescent-cardboard.com

Cretacolor
www.cretacolor.com

Daler-Rowney USA Ltd.
Cranbury, NJ; (609) 655-5252
www.daler-rowney.com

Daniel Smith
Seattle, WA; (800) 426-7923
www.danielsmith.com

Da Vinci Brushes
(See Gregory Daniels
Fine Arts)

Da Vinci Paint Company
Irvine, CA; (800) 553-8755
www.davincipaints.com

DecoArt, Inc.
Stanford, KY
(800) 367-3047 ext. 3146
www.decoart.com

Delta Technical
Coatings, Inc.
Whittier, CA; (800) 423-4135
www.deltacrafts.com

Dick Blick Art Materials
Galesburg, IL; (800) 828-4548
www.dickblick.com

Dr. Ph. Martin's
(See Salis International Inc.)

Dynasty
Glendale, NY; (718) 821-5939
www.dynasty-brush.com

Fredrix
Lawrenceville, GA
www.fredrixartistcanvas.com

FW Artists' Inks
(See Daler-Rowney USA Ltd.)

Gamblin Artists Colors Co.
Portland, OR; (502) 235-1945
www.gamblincolors.com

General Pencil Company
Redwood City, CA
(650) 369-4889
www.generalpencil.com

Gessobord
(See Ampersand Art Supply)

Golden Artist Colors, Inc.
New Berlin, NY
(800) 959-6543
www.goldenpaints.com

Gregory Daniels Fine Arts
Glendale, CA; (877) 862-8892
www.gdfa.net

Grumbacher
(See Sanford Brands)

Gruppo Maimeri
Milano, Italy
Tel: ++ 39 (2) 906981
www.maimeri.it

Holbein Works, Ltd.
www.holbein-works.co.jp

Isabey
(See Cheap Joe's Art Stuff or
Dick Blick Art Materials)

Iwata Medea Inc.
Portland, OR; (503) 253-7308
www.iwata-medea.com

Jack Richeson &
Company, Inc.
Kimberly, WI; (800) 233-2404
www.richesonart.com

JansenArt
www.jansenarttraditions.com

Lanaquarelle
(See Dick Blick Art Materials)

Liquitex
(See ColArt Americas, Inc.)

Loew-Cornell, Inc.
Englewood Cliffs, NJ
(201) 836-7070
www.loew-cornell.com

M. Graham & Co.
West Linn, OR; (503) 656-6761
www.mgraham.com

MaimeriBlu
(See Gruppo Maimeri)

Martin/F. Weber Company
Philadelphia, PA
(215) 677-5600
www.weberart.com

Masquepen
(800) 947-1389
www.masquepen.com

Masterson Art Products
Phoenix, AZ; (800) 965-2675
www.mastersonart.com

Princeton Art and Brush
Company
Princeton, NJ; (609) 683-1122
www.princetonartandbrush.
com

Prismacolor
(See Sanford Brands)

Robert Simmons Brushes
(See Daler-Rowney USA Ltd.)

Royal Brush Manufacturing,
Inc. (Royal & Langnickel)
Merrillville, IN
(800) 247-2211
www.royalbrush.com

Royal Talens B.V.
The Netherlands
Tel: +31 (55) 527 4700
www.talens.com

Salis International Inc.
Golden, CO; (800) 843-8293
www.docmartins.com

Sanford Brands
(800) 323-0749
www.sanford.com
www.grumbacherart.com
www.prismacolor.com

Saral Paper Corp.
New York, NY
(212) 223-3322
www.saralpaper.com

Scharff Brushes, Inc.
www.artbrush.com

Sherry C. Nelson brushes
www.sherrycnelson.com

Silver Brush Limited
Windsor, NJ; (609) 443-4900
www.silverbrush.com

Strathmore Artist Paper
Westfield, MA
(800) 353-0375
www.strathmoreartist.com

Sumi Ink
(See Cheap Joe's Art Stuff or
Dick Blick Art Materials)

Van Gogh
(See Royal Talens B.V.)

Winsor & Newton
www.winsornewton.com

Zhen Studio
P.O. Box 33142
Reno, NV 89533
lianzhen@yahoo.com
(Send a letter or an email with
your inquiry.)

Index

Learn to paint delightful, realistic animals with these other fine North Light Books!

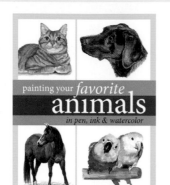

Fine artists and decorative painters alike will relish Claudia Nice's easy-to-follow, conversational instruction. *Painting Your Favorite Animals in Pen, Ink and Watercolor* includes 14 complete step-by-step projects that teach how to refine simple shapes into drawings, add color and finish with pen and ink, as well as over 60 mini-demos that teach how to capture eyes, ears, tails, feet, fur and feathers, with each final work portraying realistic animal movements. Study an amazing range of dogs, sheep, parakeets, cows, pigs, cats and wild horses!

ISBN-13: 978-1-58180-776-9, ISBN-10: 1-58180-776-7, Hardcover, 144 pages, #33447

With *Painting Animal Friends*, it's possible to paint cats, dogs, horses, ducks and more without any fine art training at all! There are over 27 demonstrations of the most popular animals, each with a template line drawing to help you get started right away.

ISBN-13: 978-1-58180-598-7, ISBN-10: 1-58180-598-5, Paperback, 128 pages, #33111

From a perfectly posed butterfly to a delicately tinted leaf to tiny eggs in a bird's nest, realistic natural details enhance a painting's appeal. Internationally acclaimed artist and teacher Peggy Harris shares her secrets with tips, demonstrations and fascinating facts, showing you how to observe nature accurately and let your own knowledge give credibility to your art. Let *Painting Nature* inspire your imagination while giving you the techniques you need to paint attractive and convincing nature scenes. See and paint nature as never before!

ISBN-13: 978-1-58180-715-8, ISBN-10: 1-58180-715-5, Paperback, 128 pages, #33382

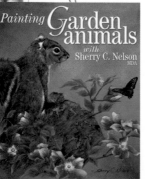

Author of the best-selling *Painting Garden Birds* and *Painting Flowers A to Z*, Sherry C. Nelson is known for her innovative and creative methods for painting animals in oils and acrylics. *Painting Garden Animals* gives decorative painters a chance to learn methods through detailed step-by-step instruction. Learn to paint those animals we know and love—a curious kitten, a furry yellow chick, a playful squirrel—from one of the most beloved artists and teachers in the industry!

ISBN-13: 978-1-58180-427-0, ISBN-10: 1-58180-427-X, Paperback, 144 pages, #32591

These books and other fine North Light titles are available at your local fine art retailer or bookstore or from online suppliers.